SPRING JAUNTS

SPRING JAUNTS

SOME WALKS, EXCURSIONS

& PERSONAL EXPLORATIONS

OF TOWN, COUNTRY & SEASHORE

ANTHONY BAILEY

FARRAR, STRAUS & GIROUX

NEW YORK

To Margot, especially

Contents

Preface

I WROTE these pieces over a long period. The reader is therefore offered no guarantee that every detail is the same now as when I first noticed it, walking by. The ferries to the Isle of Wight sail these days under different colors; the names of some of New Hampshire's coastal motels and restaurants have undoubtedly changed; and on the Côte d'Azur, where sun-belt development proceeds at more than a walking pace, at least one casino that I mentioned has gone out of business. Possibly the Boyne Valley in Ireland has altered somewhat less. And the Severn, scene of my journey with a coracle, can be excluded from this apology, since my observations on it are relatively up-to-date.

I have always thought of these pieces as spring jaunts, but as I assembled them for this book I realized that not all of them took place in spring. It was the mood of spring that impelled me rather than dates in the calendar. The mood can take me at other times, with a need for fresh pastures, different air in the lungs, new sights to see. Sometimes I walked forth with an optimistic, renovatory impulse—as if to go crusading—and sometimes in the hope of finding en route a spot like that encountered by

Preface

William Cobbett: "one of those pretty, clean, unstenched, unconfined places that tend to lengthen life and make it happy." Or I may have set out with the thought of running across people or events that might give life for a moment a dash of meaning and intensity. Spring feelings.

All of these pieces first appeared in slightly different form in *The New Yorker*, to whose editors and editorial staff I am, as always, grateful. "Irish Miles" has also appeared in *Acts of Union*, a collection of my reports on Ireland published by Random House, but it seems to belong equally in this company.

THE ISLE OF WIGHT!

THE ISLE OF WIGHT!

caused all the cups of tea in the first- and third-class saloons to take a sudden jump, to lie still for a moment as the captain considered what to do, and then to begin vibrating again as the pistons went in and out and the wheels thrashed in reverse.

Ferries (now twin-screw and diesel-driven) still run. There is also a newer service of Hovercraft, built by an Isle of Wight firm, which make the crossing in seven minutes, and I took one of these vehicles on this occasion. It looked like a single-decker bus fixed to the top half of a whale. Pushed by an aircraft propeller and kept several feet aloft by a fan, which creates air pressure inside a thick rubber skirt between the craft's hull and the water, the Hovercraft dashed with a buzzing, chain-saw noise and a mushy, limousine-like motion across Spithead. The March morning was clear, but spray flew in thick sheets past the windows. There was no view. The twenty passengers looked at each other for their reactions. Then the driver, who had a veteran RAF fighter-pilot mustache, throttled back, and the machine climbed Ryde beach like a fat crocodile, scattering shingle, and finally —as if punctured—settled slowly with all its engines cut.

We had landed next to Ryde Station, which is at the shore end of Ryde Pier. I stopped for a moment to watch the crowd that had just landed from the ordinary ferry: Boy Scouts, salesmen, elderly couples looking for a retirement home, a soldier on leave, a honeymoon pair, women with children, an old man with a dog, and, at the last, three men who seemed linked together as they climbed into a waiting dark-blue van. I had begun to walk uphill through Ryde town when it struck me that these men must have been two police officers and a convict bound for Parkhurst, the prison near the center of the island—a rough piece of the present to consider in the midst of what might otherwise be thought of as wholly pastoral, late-Romantic, and ideal.

Take Ryde: despite a Wimpy hamburger joint and a few pseudo-modern shopfronts, it is still an early-nineteenth-century watering place. Ryde's success started the Isle of Wight in the resort trade. According to *The Buildings of England: Hampshire and the Isle of Wight* (a volume in an incomparable architectural guide, covering most of Britain, edited and generally written by Nikolaus Pevsner), the town's population was six hundred in 1795 and three thousand in 1821. Pevsner finds the buildings of Ryde dull. (Henry Fielding, whose vessel put in there for shelter on his voyage to Lisbon, was similarly not much taken with it—his mood colored by bad weather, perhaps, and by his landlady. She impressed the author of *Tom Jones* as more concerned with scrubbing floors than with feeding Henry Fielding.) Moreover, Ryde is a sudden introduction to the fatiguing fact that most of the island coastal towns are hilly. Union Street, with a gradient of about one in seven, has been craftily made one-way downhill for motor vehicles, but for me, on the sidewalk, it was all uphill, past Yelf's Hotel and the Royal Victoria Arcade ("Italianate front, Doric pilasters. Original shops and lantern lighting inside . . . extremely attractive," says Pevsner, in a rare ray of Ryde sunshine). The Arcade was now empty except for a betting shop and, according to a real-estate agent's sign, was awaiting serious inquiries. I spotted several sporting types entering the bookie's in order to make serious inquiries about the day's racing form. If William Gilbert (whose spirit is in the air in Ryde) were alive today, he should write an operetta about a go-ahead bookmaker in the down-at-heel Royal Victoria Arcade. Chorus: "Italianate front, Doric pilasters."

Whistling a snatch from *Pinafore*, I turned west through St. Thomas's Square, past the town hall, with its columns (Ionic above and Tuscan below, according to Pevsner), and past a new development of detached houses built in the native sandy Isle of Wight stone. Apart from a blustery northeasterly wind, it was a fine day. I stopped at the entrance to Ryde's nine-hole golf course to choose a path that would start me counter-clockwise around the island, along the north shore—with the wind, if not quite at my back, at least behind my right shoulder. I was carrying a canvas satchel, which contained a plastic raincoat, a change of clothes, Pevsner, and Ordnance Survey Sheet 180, a map scaled one inch to one statute mile, with clear detail on the minutiae of landscape: rivulets, quarries, windmills, tall chimneys, bus depots, churches, Roman villas, and notable pubs (such as the Hare & Hounds at Arreton, where the last island public hanging took place), all held together in a skein of red and yellow roads, gray towns, light green woods, and orange contours. On the island, as the map indicates, there is a network of footpaths, a few paved, some muddy, many signposted. I took one that ran between hedges across the links. A female foursome stood, with slapping skirts, waiting to drive from the first tee. The path became a lane in Binstead Village and then a path again through a copse, where, at my coming, a squirrel—notable because it was a red squirrel—ran up a tree. The Isle of Wight is the last British refuge of the red squirrel: the gray variety, which generally drives out its red cousins, doesn't seem to have made the crossing yet. Through a half-open gate, I came into the meadows of Quarr Abbey.

There are in fact two Quarr Abbeys, old and new. For four hundred years, from 1131, a Cistercian monastery was the main civilizing influence on the island—a historian's verdict that gains added weight when you know that in the fifteenth century the abbot had his own ships for bringing in duty-free wine. Times changed. The sixteenth-century topographer Lambarde wrote: "The inhabitants of this island be wont to boast merrily that they neither had amongst them monks, lawyers, wolves nor foxes, yet I find them all save one in a monastery called Quarr." The monastery was dissolved in 1537. Pevsner describes what is left of it: a gray "Early Victorian Cottage with C13 [thirteenth-century] motifs," standing "against a big barn, the drive-in bay of which has a group of genuine C13 tall stepped lancets reset." He adds, "This is one of the few aesthetically rewarding details on the site." The rest is more confusing, with a great deal shifted around in Cs 18 and 19 for picturesque reasons. "What e.g. is the meaning of the arch with a slight continuous chamfer, and of the wall standing higher near it?" Pevsner asks peevishly.

Beneath the south windows of the cottage, anenomes were coming up, and crocuses were appearing under a hedge. I took a lane westward through the grounds of the abbey, which had been resettled by French Benedictines in the nineteenth century; the new abbey buildings could be glimpsed among the trees to the north. Bells rang in a brash terra-cotta-colored tower—unattractive Belgian brick, says Pevsner, for whom, however, the buildings are a virtuoso performance. The architect was Dom Paul Bellot. "He should appear in books in the line of descent of the early Gaudí of the Casa Vicens and then of Berlage and de Klerk and of Hoeger in Germany." The church, built in 1911–12, has Catalan motifs, while the gable of the nearby abbey rises in steps, like that of houses in Amsterdam. The effect of the buildings was strong, though for me diluted by the trees, and not at all displeasing. No monks were visible. In their stead, a herd of Friesian cows ambled up to a hedge and peered at me in a friendly fashion as I walked by. The lane turned into a bumpy road, going downhill to Wootton Creek.

The ferry at Wootton carries cars to and from the mainland, and to cross the creek I detoured inland half a mile to the main Ryde–Cowes road, making a swift passage through the unprepossessing between-the-wars ribbon-development village. Then I turned off on a minor road leading through Blanket Copse to Whipping-ham and Osborne—a dull section, though it may have seemed so because the wind was sharper, on my right cheek rather than over my right shoulder, and the sun had gone behind an extensive mat of cloud. Light is a serious part of landscape; that of the Isle of Wight is, for England, positively southern, the light of Turner rather than of Constable. Walking here in 1850, some years before he became a landscape architect, the American farmer Frederick Law Olmsted wrote: "Beauty, grandeur, impressiveness in any way, from scenery, is not often to be found in a few prominent, distinguishable features, but in the manner and the unobserved materials with which these are connected and combined. Clouds, light, states of the atmosphere, and circumstances that we cannot always detect, affect all landscapes, and especially landscapes in which the vicinity of a body of water is an element." When he first reached the island, Olmsted thought it "more dreary, desolate, bare and monotonous, than any equal extent of land you probably ever saw in America—would be, rather, if it were not that you are rarely out of sight of the sea." Soon he was talking of downland, the bright dells, the craggy south shore, "the majesty of vastness," and the cottages, most of which were "quiet, cosy, ungenteel, yet elegant," adding to rather than insulting "the natural charm of their neighborhood." There were exceptions, especially among the later erections, but Olmsted tactfully didn't say whether he put Osborne in this sorry category. Passing the country retreat of Queen Victoria and her consort —by no means a cosy cottage—he saw only the top of a campanile, and reflected on the unstately manner in which the Royal Family lived there, when it could. "The Prince himself turns farmer, and engages with much ardor in improving the agricultural capabilities of the soil . . . The Prince is well known as a successful breeder and stock-farmer, having taken several prizes for fat cattle, etc., at the great annual shows. Her Majesty . . . is in the habit of driving herself a pair of ponies, unattended, through the estate, studying the comfort of her little cottage tenantry, and in every way she can trying to seem to herself the goodwife of a respectable country gentleman."

I didn't do a lot better than Olmsted in seeing Osborne. He was prevented by the family's being in residence, and I by the fact that the government caretakers close the house and grounds from the end of October to the beginning of April. However, assuming an inspectorial air, and trying to look obsessed with rhododendrons and kitchen gardens, I marched up the empty drive and presently found myself faced with Osborne House, whose source, writes Pevsner, "is the villas in the paintings of Claude Lorraine." But whereas in the scale of a painting, and suffused in the romantic light which pervades the paintings of Claude, such villas are well and good, here on an early March English day they are not; Osborne is ugly. Two three-story wings form an L. Each wing has a campanile, with deep eaves. There is a Germanic heaviness, and one is not surprised to learn that the poet, painter, and farmer Prince Consort was also—with the assistance of the eminent London builder Thomas Cubitt —an architect. Albert and his wife paid for Osborne themselves; it was to be their refuge from public life.

They went there twice a year, from the end of December to the end of January, and from mid-July to the end of August. And it was to Osborne, at King Leopold of the Belgians' suggestion, that Victoria retreated on Albert's death, in 1861 (of typhoid, at Windsor). In the evenings, she had his dinner clothes laid out. Over the royal bed hung a painting of him lying in state, and by her pillow a small easel portrait she could turn to, waking up. In the grounds, a miniature earthwork fort called the Albert Barracks provided room for the children to work off their martial energies. A scaled-down cottage and vegetable patch were there for the domestic and agricultural instincts. As for life in the interior (where in 1890 the Durbar Room was added, under the supervision of Bhai Ram Singh and John Lockwood Kipling, the poet's father, with sixty feet of carved teak paneling, Indian columns, and an ornamental plaster peacock), the atmosphere was a good bit Indian Army and a little bit Kafka, at least from the point of view of young Marie Mallet, a lady-in-waiting. She wrote (in a letter to her stepsister that has been published in a collection of her letters by John Murray, London):

The most annoying part of this life is that mere nothings are shrouded in deep mystery, and one never knows what is going to happen till a few minutes before it comes off; I suppose one gets accustomed to it in time, but at first it is most tiresome. We had rather a gay evening yesterday. The Maharajah of

Kuch Behar dined with the Queen and a very good band came from Portsmouth to enliven the feast. I dined with the household, but at ten we were all marched into the drawing room and were stared at as usual until ¼ to 11, when the Queen having been safely seen upstairs, we adjourned to the council room and danced on a carpet! to the sound of a piano mecanique turned alternatively by the Duchess of Albany and Col. Carington. It really was very comical. Prince Henry [of Battenberg] got tremendously excited and pranced about all over the place, he nearly whirled me off my legs, for he dances in the German fashion and plunges horribly.

It was downhill into East Cowes, a scrappy collection of houses, factories, and boatyards on the east bank of the Medina River. The Medina rises in the downs very near the southern point of the island, and flows northward through Newport (the centrally situated market town which serves as the island's capital), where it becomes a broad and, at low tide, muddy estuary for the last five miles to Cowes. From the chain ferry that took me across the river, I could see on the East Cowes shore the huge cocooned bulk of a Princess flying boat, half in and half out of a waterfront hangar, the last British attempt to produce a giant passenger-carrying plane that also had the ability to land on and take off from water. Having had no luck with the Princess, the Isle of Wight is doing much better with Hovercraft, which don't get quite so far off the water.

In any event, as Stratford is Shakespeare, or Manchester cotton, Cowes is boats. From my room at the Gloster Hotel I looked out over the mouth of the Medina. Out in the Solent, large ships passed on their way to Southampton. To my left, along the promenade, I could make out a tower of the Royal Yacht Squadron's headquarters, on the site of a castle of Henry VIII, a gloomy building whose restored fortifications look scarcely adequate for keeping out the wrong sort of people. The Royal Yacht Squadron was founded in 1815, the year of Waterloo, and did not let in Sir Thomas Lipton until his eighty-first year. But there are numerous other clubs in Cowes, and the salt democratically dispersed in every Englishman's blood is quite evident for a week each August when five or six hundred small craft congregate there to joust with each other, the weather, and the tricky Solent tides. At Yarmouth, ten miles along the northwest shore of the island, the harbor master in summer often puts up a sign at the entrance breakwater: "Harbor Full." Now, in early March, a single small white cruising sloop with tanned sails fetched slowly along the shore against the northeasterly, while a racing-dinghy enthusiast in yellow foul-weather gear planed back and forth across the river mouth.

I had dinner on the *Medway Queen*, a paddle-wheel ferry steamer that has been converted into a club and restaurant and is moored in a former millpond a few miles up the Medina. In prewar summers, the *Medway Queen* carried passengers on the Thames Estuary. In May 1940, she made seven trips to the Dunkirk beaches, rescuing seven thousand troops and all the crew and soldiers aboard another paddler, the *Brighton Belle*, which had sunk. None of the old Isle of Wight paddlers was rescued from the breaker's yard, but the *Medway Queen* furnishes an upstanding example of the type—plumb-stemmed and flush-decked, with a skinny twenty-five-foot-high yellow funnel, sharply raked aft, and an open bridge lined with brass handrails and white canvas dodgers. The white wooden paddle boxes are elegantly made, with the ship's name set into the curved top, and the crest of her first owners—a white horse rampant—

surrounded by scrollwork over the hub of the paddle wheel. Below, the engine room can be seen from open alleyways. The engine frames are painted bright green, the pistons, rods, and cranks are polished steel, and the controls and steam gauges are shining brass and copper. There is checkered steel plating underfoot. Without much difficulty, you can imagine steam whistling up from the cylinders, bells ringing, the handles of the engine-room telegraph moving, and then the pistons going slowly in and out and the long polished arms cranking the paddle wheels round. Coming to the island as a child, I would watch this and then run up the companionways to stand on deck behind the funnel out of the wind or perch on one of the seats that looked like rolltop desks and also served, if needed, as life rafts. The decks were of pine laid over steel and caulked rather sloppily with black tar. Approaching Ryde Pier, I used to watch the lad who had the job of heaving the line used—by men on the pier—to haul up the first mooring warp. He had a dedicated expression, and wore black boots, navy trousers, and a coarse black turtleneck sweater with the words "Southern Railway" curved across his chest in red.

In the fo'c'sle restaurant of the *Medway Queen*, I had a rump steak, chips, and peas, and lost fifty pence in one of the one-arm bandits that here, as elsewhere in Britain (where taxes and gambling seem to rise in direct ratio), are increasing the profits of clubs, pubs, and hotels. Back at the Gloster, I had a nightcap in the saloon bar, open to nonresidents of the hotel. Two men, one wearing a sheepskin motoring coat, the other a brown mackintosh, stood at the bar, while a plump-faced, well-dressed woman, perhaps the wife of one of them, sat in a nearby chair.

"But I would never *knowingly* employ a socialist," said the man in the sheepskin coat. "I would never pay out money to nurture socialism."

"But what about Malcolm?" asked his wife, who was drinking a gin and tonic.

"Malcolm?"

"Yes, don't you like Malcolm?"

"Oh, old Muggeridge," said the man, in the way people have of making television personalities sound as if they are close friends.

"Yes, don't you like him?"

"Oh, he's all right, he's come round a lot lately."

The man in the mackintosh said, "But now, what about this new law, all this about consenting males? If you ask me, the only way to the top in some jobs is going to be through consenting males. Country's riddled with it."

"I don't know," said sheepskin. "Doesn't worry me. Anyway, aren't they all going to Russia? Russia's going queer."

The woman said, "You know what old Malcolm said the other night about Christianity?" But apparently both of them did know, and the conversation lapsed while the man in the raincoat ordered another round of drinks.

The northeaster had dropped next morning. I set out after an inspiring Gloster breakfast of porridge, eggs, bacon, sausage, toast, chunky marmalade, and coffee, served by an affable young Italian waiter—most of the hotel staff on the island are Italian and Spanish. The sun, without stirring one to Mediterranean comparisons, pierced a thin tissue of cloud, behind which the sky was watercolor blue. I walked past the premises of the Royal Yacht Squadron and along the stone-walled Princes

Esplanade, built, according to a plaque, "by the West Cowes Board of Health, A.D. 1894." Another sign said that football, cricket, and horse riding were prohibited. Then the mid- and late-Victorian houses suddenly stopped, and past a pink marine beacon, the Solent stretched away to the mainland, here marked by the three-hundred-foot-high chimney of a power station. To judge from the tilt of a buoy off Egypt Point, the tide was rushing east. Small waves sucked and splashed between moss- and seaweed-covered rocks. A group of men, wearing the tieless shirts, pullovers, and old suit jackets favored by British laborers, were working at the end of the footpath. I had to head inland, past some pretty horrible little corrugated-iron bungalows, several converted railway carriages, and small houses covered with the stucco pebble dash that was the popular between-the-wars facing material. This conglomeration, the whole less beautiful even than the parts, was Gurnard. I noted one property called Erz an Myne and another called Happieshack. Some people were walking dogs, and one young Gurnard matron proudly pushed her child along in a stroller while the nipper, leaning out, impeded progress by dragging its hand on the top of one wheel.

Beyond Gurnard, I climbed a footpath to some clifftop fields, but the path came to an end at the cliff edge. I marched south for a mile or so. A westerly fork brought me right through a muddy farm, where two milkmaids, quite fetching in white smocks and boots, were moving milk churns into a shed. And then, abruptly, I was on top of a rise looking south toward the interior of the island: green fields with white gulls and black crows sitting in them; the dark woods of Parkhurst forest; and farther distant, the range of downs, now patchily illuminated by shafts of light that fell dramatically from a thick group of curdling creamy-gray clouds. What British forecasters term a "bright" day had quickly become what they call "unsettled" and was on the way to becoming "showery." Two schoolboys bicycled past, wearing blue gabardine raincoats of a kind I remembered as being not altogether waterproof. I donned my black lightweight plastic mac. Rain fell for a minute, and afterward the air was sweet with it—it hung in the grass verges and bramble hedges. As I climbed the next hill, a second shower fell, big drops this time splashing me in the face while the sun shone in the fields beyond.

Squalls off the island have been the ruination of several ships—like the *Royal George*, which went down off the Isle of Wight with eight hundred men in 1783, or like *H.M.S. Eurydice*, which foundered off the southern tip, St. Catherine's Point, in March 1878, with the loss of some three hundred lives. She was homeward bound from Bermuda, with her gunports open, under full sail. Watching her from the cliffs was the young Winston Spencer Churchill, who recalled being rushed to shelter from the sudden squall. When he looked again, three masts were all that could be seen of the *Eurydice*. Gerard Manley Hopkins (who used to stay at Freshwater, toward the western end of the island) recorded the weather and its effect:

> *Now Carisbrook keep goes under in gloom;*
> *Now it overvaults Appledurcombe;*
> > *Now near by Ventnor town*
> *It hurls, hurls off Boniface Down.*
>
> *Too proud, too proud, what a press she bore!*
> *Royal, and all her royals wore.*
> > *Sharp with her, shorten sail!*
> *Too late; lost; gone with the gale.*

My road passed through a wood; tall trees with a northeasterly tilt and, in their tops, a rookery, full of noisy, gregarious black birds with ragged wings. Then Porchfield, which was a few houses, a small, run-down stone Bethel Chapel (1849), with an overgrown graveyard, and a pleasant-looking pub, the Sportsman's Rest, which offered neither beer nor rest just then, being shut. My own view of the British licensing laws is that they do less to protect the populace from early drunkenness than to safeguard the late rising of pub landlords. I halted at the junction of the Cowes–Newport–Yarmouth roads, where in a small patch of green turf an old ship's timber had been set, a blackened oak rib inscribed "In Grateful Memory of the Men from Porchfield and Newtown who fell in the Great War 1914–1919." It was a refreshing change from the expensive stone slabs to be seen in some towns—the sort that look like headstones put up by heirs to a rich uncle they'd never really known. I think of my father's former neighbor, Mr. Stanley Powell, a veteran of the trenches, the most good-humored of elderly men, who never got over his disdain for those who were at home during that war. "It was another world. They had no idea."

I strode along a minor road that paralleled one of the muddy arms of Newtown Harbor, and was suddenly bumped into by a large four-legged something which bounded out of a hedge—a Great Dane, about four feet high and six feet long, pursued by a large man, about six feet tall and ample with fury, who clambered across the ditch and yelled, "Jane! Jane! Come here, old girl! Come here, you bloody bitch. Jane! Jane! *Jane*." His voice, somewhat exhausted, found a soothing note, and he stood with his hands on his waist while the dog ran up and down the road, out of reach. Presently a girl rode up on a motor scooter and blocked the road in one direction, while the man attempted to close in on the dog. Sometimes Jane ran toward the girl and sometimes toward me, and didn't seem to have much trouble in eluding her pursuer. "It's the second time she's got out this morning," said the man, during a second pause to get his breath back. "She's just a puppy." After a while, Jane ran back through the hedge and the man went after her.

Newtown is the sort of place many people find dismal. The smell of marsh and mud envelops the village, which lies at the head of a network of creeks, and there is an ever-present note of promise come to naught—through French attacks, lack of people, and the silting up of its once-prosperous harbor. Roads were laid out for development of a new town in the eighteenth century, but today there are no more than fifteen houses. The most prominent building is the town hall, built in 1699, a nicely proportioned brick-and-stone structure, with a columned portico and a sign declaring it to be "the meeting place of the Mayor and Corporation of the Burgesses of Newtown and until the passing of the Reform Act 1832, the setting of many parliamentary elections." Until the passing of the Reform Act, Newtown (like many another rotten borough) sent two members to Parliament. There are still two mail collections a day from the red postbox, inscribed "VR" for "Victoria Regina," which is set into the wall of one of the houses. An oyster fishery has existed at Newtown since Roman times, but a fierce winter a few years ago decimated 500,000 oysters. Some shellfish farmers have now turned to clams, which were discovered in England after the war, and for which they have found a ready market in Paris and in London hotels frequented by Americans.

Through a gate, I found myself on a path leading across a sodden meadow to a little dike across the marsh. In places the dike became a wooden jetty, with a shaky handrail on one side alone. Two men in blue jerseys and waist-high wading boots passed me on one section of the jetty. I held on to the rail while they edged by, giving me friendly nods that seemed to acknowledge our common, precarious fate. The jetty led to an island, grass verged and underpinned with stone, surrounded by oyster ponds. There was a small weather-boarded boathouse. South, over the downs, gray-white puffs of cloud reared skyward, and the sun shone on lush green fields, framed with the darker green strokes of hedges. In the channels between the marsh islands, water moved beneath some moored boats and lapped against a pair of clinker dinghies pulled up by the boathouse, while the light breeze stirred the grass on the islands and hummocks and fields. I sat on an old piece of timber and listened to the sounds.

Lunchtime found me at the New Inn, in Shalfleet, the village at the western corner of Newtown Harbor. The New Inn, built in the fifteenth century, was devoid of customers, but the publican served me a pint of cool draft bitter (a lot of nonsense is talked about warm English beer; a good pub has its kegs in a cold cellar) and then produced from his kitchen a stack of tasty ham sandwiches. I sat in front of a coal fire and found company in the weekly Isle of Wight *County Press*. Local crime seemed to consist of a few cases of dangerous driving, some petty theft, and one case of sugar in a gas tank. The real-estate market was prosperous, with a long column of houses wanted. Island industry seemed to be doing well, particularly Britten-Norman, a small firm building light aircraft, which had just got a big export order for a model called the Islander. The workmen were giving up vacation time to build the planes. One worker said he liked doing a job where he could see what he was making from start to finish. I was also pleased to see the name of Bailey's, the drapery firm started by my great-grandfather and now run by my father's younger brother, Jim. At their Sandown, Shanklin, and Cowes stores, an advertisement declared, Bailey's was having a sale of winter woollies.

I spent the afternoon walking from Shalfleet to Alum Bay, near the western extremity of the island. For three and a half miles I was on the main road, out of sight of the water, and the chief items of interest were an owl, hooting in the woods near Bouldnor, several Minis whipping round the bends at sixty m.p.h., and an out-of-season mystery bus tour carrying a party of old ladies around some of the island beauty spots, with stops for chatter and tea. These tours are a commercial version of a Sunday-afternoon drive with mother-in-law, and the mystery lies in the fact that no set route is announced, thus increasing the frequency of Oohs, Aahs, and Oh, what lovely scenery! The increasing number and speed of cars, and the naïveté of the local wildlife, may have accounted for the number of dead birds and hedgehogs that I passed. Walking slowly past these squashed remains is much different from driving past them.

Yarmouth is a town of nice rooftops. In the dark church, I stopped to look at the pink-and-gray marble effigy of Sir Robert Holmes, the Irish freebooter whom Charles II made governor of the island after Holmes had had a successful career of harrying the Dutch. Holmes was a leader of the expedition that seized Nieuw Amsterdam in 1664 and rechristened it—with tactful affection for Charles Stuart and his brother the Duke of York—New York. I would have stopped at Holmes's old home, the George Hotel, but it was closed for the season, and I strolled on, past the harbor and across a bridge which cuts off the harbor from the inner reaches of the River Yar. (An example of insularity, if you like: the island has three rivers, one called the Medina, the other two called Yar—the eastern Yar debouches at Bembridge; the western Yar, naturally enough, at Yarmouth.) Until 1863, there was a ferry across the river, charging a penny for a workingman and sixpence for any gentleman wearing a white collar. The bridge is free.

I followed a path across fields to Colwell Bay and the village of Totland, a shabby-genteel region of bungalows, holiday chalets, caravan camps, and boarding houses, whose quintessential expression is the Needles Tea Bar at Alum Bay. The Needles are worn chalk pinnacles that form the ragged western point of the island. Alum Bay, just east of them, is an open demonstration of six geological strata, but its rainbow-striped cliffs, said to be vivid on a sunny day after heavy rain, were not particularly so on this occasion. Yellow, rose, and gray were all I made out in the cliffs themselves. Alum was once dug there, and at the Tea Bar you can now buy, along with picture postcards and garden ornaments in the shape of gnomes and fairies, plastic containers which (for five pence) you can fill with colored sands from handily placed trays at the cliff top. Here I boarded a bus. By a roundabout route which included Newport and passed the front gate of Parkhurst Prison, it brought me back to Cowes and the Gloster, in time for a restorative drink and dinner.

My father was born and grew up above the family dairy in Shanklin, and although he and my mother now live on the Hampshire mainland, a few miles from the Solent, he feels the call of the island two or three times a year. Early next morning he drove me out to Alum Bay. I arranged to meet him that evening at the Savoy Hotel in Shanklin, just round the southern corner of the island; then I set off up the one-in-two north face of Tennyson Down. This is near the western end of the hills that run all the way across the island. I climbed diagonally, occasionally using a well-anchored clump of grass for a handhold. At the top, the wind restored my breath. The top was only a hundred yards or so broad, and fell away sharply on both sides: on the cliff side to the south, four hundred and fifty sheer feet to the sea; on the northern scarp side, sharply enough to put Totland and Freshwater in what the British Army calls "dead ground"—meaning that what is down there is hidden, and that if a machine gun were fired, it would go over the heads of soldiers or over the chimneys of the horrible bungalows. Although the southwest wind was strong, I found as I sauntered close to the cliff edge that there was a small vacuum there; for the wind hits the steep cliffs and flies up over them. However, the word "saunter," I seem to remember from Thoreau, is derived from the French crusading cry "*A la Sainte Terre!*" and having no desire to go to the Holy Land or anywhere else at that moment, I backed into the wind again after a glimpse of light-green water breaking white on white rocks and dark shoal patches down below.

On the summit of the down is a stone Saxon-type cross, with a lightning rod at its top, a beacon to mariners and a monument to Alfred Lord Tennyson, raised "by the people of Freshwater and other friends in England and America."

TENNYSON

BORN AUGUST 6, 1809

DIED OCTOBER 6, 1892

There is also a National Trust collection box; a compass rose giving directions to Ushant (241 miles), the D Day beaches (102 miles), and London (88 miles); and on this sort of clear, breezy day, a view of everywhere. To the east stretched the island downs:

> *The hills are shadows, and they flow*
> *From form to form, and nothing stands:*
> *They melt like mist, the solid lands,*
> *Like clouds they shape themselves and go.*

Tennyson moved to the Isle of Wight in 1853, seeking seclusion. Three years earlier, at the age of forty-one, he had been appointed Poet Laureate. With the profits of poetry (*Enoch Arden* sold sixty thousand copies and earned him six thousand pounds in one year), he bought a big Georgian house called Farringford, between Freshwater and the down; but there fame pursued him. He was something between the Albert Schweitzer and the Frank Sinatra of his time. Gladstone came to Farringford, and so did Charles Darwin, the astronomer John Herschel, the philosophers Jowett and Maurice, the painter Watts, Jenny Lind, Arthur Sullivan, Prince Albert, Lewis Carroll, Longfellow, Lear, Edward Fitzgerald, Kingsley, and, not least, Garibaldi, the celebrated guerrilla, who planted a type of Sequoia called Wellingtonia on the Farringford lawn and discussed politics with the poet. Tennyson later told his wife that the Italian general had the "divine stupidity of a hero." Tennyson walked daily on the downs, built a studio in a field and a wooden footbridge from his garden to the studio, over a lane, so that he could avoid autograph seekers. It didn't help. "Admirers shinned up trees overlooking the house," writes Lawrence Wilson, a recent and accomplished island historian. "They climbed banks, [and] bolder spirits marched up the drive and rang the front door bell." One American family were said to have sold all they had for the journey to see the bard. He met them at the entrance to the drive, wearing his famous sombrero and cape, and dismissing their hopes of a welcome with an oracular "This may not be!"

For a hundred years, the island was a close-at-hand Mykonos, an English Ischia. Wordsworth came for a month in the summer of 1793 and left with melancholy forebodings that the conflict with the French would go on for a long time. Keats stayed for two lengthy periods during his few years of poetic maturity. Only Byron, singing the praises of the Isles of Greece, was lacking. Swinburne grew up on the Isle of Wight and was buried at Bonchurch, near Ventnor. Philip Worsley, translator of Homer, died of consumption at Freshwater (rather ignored by the Tennysons). Macaulay came. Dickens liked and then disliked Shanklin. Darwin began the first draft of *Origin of Species* while at Sandown. And even in the 1930s Auden wrote, in a poem to Christopher Isherwood:

> *August for the people and their favourite islands . . .*

> *Nine years ago, upon that southern island*
> *Where the wild Tennyson became a fossil,*
> *Half-boys, we spoke of books and praised*
> *The acid and austere, behind us only*
> *The stuccoed suburb and expensive school.*

in the shapely-figured aspect of chalk-hills in preference to those of stone, which are rugged, broken, abrupt and shapeless . . . I never contemplate these mountains without thinking I perceive something analogous to growth in their gentle swellings and smooth fungus-like protuberances, their fluted sides, and regular hollows and slopes, that carry at once the air of vegetative dilation and expansion." The chalk was laid down at least sixty million years ago when sea covered the southern half of England. At the sea's bottom accumulated an ooze made up of the armored shells of countless microscopic creatures called Foraminifera; this became chalk, and because it is a soft, porous stone, the chain of chalk which bends through England in the shape of a large pound-sterling sign has weathered into these smooth, rounded hills. The soil is shallow, the wind constant. Sheep and rabbits nibble the seedling shrubs, preventing the return of scrub and woodland, and the downland plants are hardy: sedge and thistle, and in summer wild thyme, yellow hawkweed, flax, horseshoe vetch, dropwort, harebell, gentian, sainfoin, scabious, and rampion. (I put their names down for their sounds, not because I can recognize them all.) March is early. I collected only a rough green plant a botanically minded relative called hellebore. Otherwise, for spring testimony I made do with a lark, which sang, flittering high over Brook Down, and a five-inch-long neon-brown caterpillar, which, oblivious to larks, crawled out for a sunny wriggle over my hand as I lay on my back on that down. I lay, in fact, with my back against the slope of a barrow—a long mound in which prehistoric Britons buried their dead. Looking south toward the sea, I could just make out the roof of Mottistone Manor, which was half buried by a landslip in the early eighteenth century, and which was dug out by General Jack Seely, the owner, in 1926; he found that the dryness of his kitchen was much improved by the operation. Between the pre-historic Britons and the General, people have lived in earthworks, huts, thatched cottages, castles, and villas. The Romans called the island Vectis; it is now the name of the island bus company. The word "Wight" comes from Wihtgar, a sixth-century West Saxon chieftain. Remains of earlier species are often found—strange fossils, reptiles, and amphibia. Near Sandown have been discovered the molar tooth of a mammoth and part of an iguanodon, one of the first animals to stand on its hind legs. It was twelve feet tall, a good height for dealing with the tropical vegetation (of which fossil remains have also been found).

Past a radar station on Limerstone Down I descended into Shorwell, which according to Pevsner is "a village rich in charming cottages." I passed by the cottages in favor of the Church of St. Peter. Here I sat on an oak seventeenth-century pew in the cool stone atmosphere and considered the brass plate put up by Barnabas Leigh to "two most worthie and religious gentlewomen his late deare and loyall wives Mrs. Elizabeth Bampfield who died the VIIth of March 1615 having bin ye mother of 15 hopeful children, and Mrs. Gertrude Percevall who died childles the XXII of Decemb' 1619." On the plate, Mr. Leigh's two ladies are shown standing on either side of him, each with a hand on her heart:

> *Sweet saintlike paire of soules, in whome did shine*
> *Such modells of perfection faeminine.*

My favorite island monument is in Brading Church. Carved in oak, it shows the island's most notable seven-teenth-century figure, Sir John Oglander, with florid mustaches, looking rather bored, lying on his right side with his head propped up on his arm and his legs crossed. Somewhat anachronistically, he is in full armor, with sword and shield. But Sir John strides easily over the centuries, at least in his written remains. Among the instructions he left his son George:

Marry thy daughters in time lest they marry themselves.

Suffer not thy sons to pass the Alps, for they shall learn there nothing but pride, popery or atheism.

Sir John suffered greatly from gout in the last two years of his life and invented several "excellent good recipes" for the ailment.

Take a quarter of a pound of best washing soap, and four eggs. Beat them together; spread them on a cloth, and lay it all over the place grieved.

Apply fresh oysters to the place infected, and bind them on with a cloth. Change it as the occasion serveth.

I climbed out of Shorwell on the road to Chale; it was just two o'clock. A middle-aged lady was taking a vase of daffodils into a Methodist chapel. Chickens were scratching around the yard of the house next door. The first field I came to was being plowed, and gulls and crows were settling on the newly turned soil behind the tractor. The roadside hedge had been recently clipped. I overtook two young couples, the boys perhaps fourteen, the girls a year or so younger, each boy with a shotgun under one arm and the other arm around a girl. The girls were wearing similar bell-bottom trousers, and the boys were both wearing black Wellington boots. They had a dog with them—a scruffy black dog of the kind that excites immoderate affection in its owners.

After a mile or so, I turned off at a place called Beckfield Cross and headed eastward along a muddy lane, past a farm, across fields into a broad valley. The headwaters of the Medina! Although no bridge was shown on the map, a small embankment carried the footpath across the low, wet ground. At one point, where the two-foot-wide stream trickled through a conduit, short, ivy-covered brick walls made a place to lean and look down the valley, where the stream meandered through an unprepossessing area of scrubby copse called the Wilderness. The hand of man was more visible in the ditches here, with clean mud showing on their sides, roots cut, bracken and branches stacked in neat piles, and black ash on the ground where hedges had been burned back. What we admire in countryside is not just nature but man's thoughtful direction of it. But at that moment a splendid pheasant rose, whirring, from the hedgerow—natural and glorious enough.

On a long walk, when I am going along at a settled pace, on second wind, as I was just then, whistling the few snatches I remember of Mozart's Thirty-ninth Symphony, my mind partly takes in some of the facts presented to my senses and partly freewheels on another level. A good-looking farmhouse, for instance, will set me off on a hypothetical sequence of real-estate deals, as I redistribute local property in my own favor, selling off some arable, renting out a meadow, leasing to anglers at exorbitant prices sections of riverbank, and generally enjoying to the full whatever domains I see.

I came out beyond the Wilderness on a country road (one-and-a-half cars wide) by Great Appleford Farm, whose house and buildings seemed to grow out of the ground in the same fashion as the surrounding trees. After a slight jog to the northeast, I followed a course I hoped would bring me to a disused railway line running south from Newport to Ventnor. I went north of St. Catherine's Down, the eminent (773 feet above sea level) hill in this vicinity. Under the down stand great clumps of beeches, thick black below, fanned-out gray-green-brown above. On the summit to my right I could make out the old lighthouse and the monument which commemorates the 1811 visit to England of Tsar Alexander I. But the footpath, shown on the map as reaching the old railway at Southford, went through a farmyard, and I was halted by knee-high mud and pigs' swill, an unfordable sloppy sea of it stretching forty feet from the walls of the pigsty to an earthen bank capped by barbed wire. I retreated. I took five minutes to get it off my boots, and then followed the road south again to Whitwell, a village notable for several cottages that have thatched roofs in such poor shape grass was growing on them. There, past a building site on which new bungalows were being built, past the Yarborough Arms public house, I reached the track. Or, rather, I reached the embankment on which the track had been. The railway bridge across the lane had been taken down. There were no rails or ties left, only a suspicion of a footpath, which wandered through brambles, gorse, and bracken. This track was occasionally crossed by a barbed-wire fence, under which I slithered.

Nowadays, there is only one section of the Isle of Wight railway system still open—that between Ryde, Brading, Sandown, and Shanklin. The rolling stock is obsolete equipment from the London Underground—long, electric-powered carriages, with straps for standing passengers, and springs that fail to counter the mismatched properties of carriage and track. The carriages rattle and bounce far more than those they replaced. Before the war, when I traveled on the island trains, this Newport–Ventnor line had already been abandoned, but the trains on the rest of the system were recognizably real: three small carriages, each divided into perhaps a dozen compartments, and a locomotive with a late-Victorian smokestack at one end and a coal bunker at the other, behind a cab. The cab had slanting windows at the front and portholes at the rear, for the engines ran forward up the line and—lacking turntables to spin them round—backward in the other direction. Each passenger compartment was lined with facing banks of heavily upholstered straight-backed seats, behind whose plump, stiff cushions I always as a child ran my hands, having once found a ten-shilling note. Above the seats was a handle, to be directed one way to cold, the other to hot, connected haphazardly to heating pipes under-neath. Next, set behind glass in mahogany frames, came a row of faded brown photographs depicting the delights of, say, Seaview Pier, Blackgang Chine, or Sandown High Street. Above them was a luggage rack of net strung from wrought-iron supports. In the curved ceiling, three small light bulbs glowed a dim yellow when the train passed through Wroxall tunnel. The carriage doors had handles only on the outside. To get out, you had to seize a leather strap and lift the window sash off a small sill in the centrally placed door and—giving it a simul-taneous tug toward you—let the sash down so that you could reach the outside brass handle, which always seemed stiff. Having failed to get out in time, you could resort courageously to the red emergency cord running above the windows ("Penalty for Improper Use Five Pounds"). Most of the railway system was single-track.

To avoid accidents, the engine drivers had to collect a handle from the signalman at one end of a single-track section and hand it over at the other; oncoming trains could not work the switches to enter the section without the handle. My father took the train to school in Ryde, and had to put up with a lot of joshing because en route he delivered milk from my grandfather's Shanklin dairy to his store in Ryde. When Grandfather took the train, he annoyed the engine drivers (and embarrassed my father) by never using the underground passageway between platforms but always crossing the tracks in front of the engines, at the last moment. Like the paddle-wheel ferry steamers, the engines bore the names of island towns and villages. It was my hope as a boy to ride behind each one of them—Ashey, Havenstreet, Godshill, Calbourne, Chale were the names of some—but I didn't make it, and they are gone.

Running flat, the old embankment gradually came to the level of the ground and then, as the fields rose a little, became a cutting. The track got boggy. I headed off across several fields—thickly hedged and fenced—that slanted down in one corner. I should have realized what this tilt meant: the field drained that way. But I had a nervous trespassing feeling and kept going, for the road was now visible. I began hopping from dry clod to dry clod and soon was clodhopping in a morass. My last hop landed me shin-deep in something like quicksand, but stickier. I glucked slowly forward, reaching at last the bank of a little stream and what looked like a foot-bridge, made of a single pipe, with a sign beyond it facing the road. I thought I should peer round at the sign before setting foot on the bridge. It said "11,000 Volt Cable." Well, it was perhaps well insulated, but I a terrace (the former cliff top) going inland a few hundred yards, and then the upper cliff, rising another two hundred feet. I walked along the rough, rabbit-warreny path which follows the outer edge of the terrace, first through fields, then some wild, overgrown places, and then down, past putting greens, a miniature artificial waterfall, tea gardens, and a series of little lawns with dinky green-and-yellow shelters, seats, and benches—all deserted now—into Ventnor, the generating center of this genteel cultivation. Ventnor itself clings limpet-like to the steep flank of St. Boniface Down, facing southeast, and thus sheltered from the rude southwest winds. Exotic plants bloom all winter in Ventnor. The physician Sir James Clark (who had treated Keats in Rome and had made the then excusable faulty diagnosis that the poet's problem lay in his stomach, rather than in his lungs) boosted Ventnor in the 1830s as a good place for consumptives—fresh air having replaced bleeding and a starvation diet as the proper treatment. The Royal and National Hospital for Diseases of the Chest was completed in 1871, and tiers of white, gray, and cream terraced houses, with gray slate roofs and tall chimney pots, jostled each other and intruding hotels for perches on the cliffside, while roads and pathways zigzagged between them. There is now a pier with very spindly legs and an awful ornamental triple-decker waterfall overhanging the esplanade. You need good lungs to make the ascent from that point to the old station, where the trains used to come out of the tunnel under St. Boniface Down and a bell was rung five minutes before their departure time. Young Winston Churchill stayed at 2 Verona Cottages in 1878. Karl Marx (according to Lawrence Wilson) went there in his last year of life to see if he could get rid of bronchitis and headaches. Otherwise, there is nothing in Ventnor that would make one think of either of those men.

It was gray next morning, with squalls and showers. I fed several coins into the meter for the gas fire of my room at the Savoy Hotel, in Shanklin, where I had dined with my father after taking a bus from Ventnor, and stuffed a towel under the French windows to keep out the wind and the rain. After breakfast, I talked on the telephone with my Uncle Jim, who apart from running his chain of stores is a local magistrate and chairman of the Board of Visitors at Parkhurst Prison. He suggested that, instead of going on round the edge of the island, I take a morning off and come into the center to see Parkhurst.

My uncle has a rosy, eighteenth-century sort of face, but otherwise none of the crusty qualities you would associate with the word "magistrate." In his late fifties, he drives a black MG. He parked outside Parkhurst gate and locked the car carefully. "Last week the warders told me off for leaving it unlocked," he said. "One of them said I was lucky it wasn't pinched." In fact, Parkhurst is not easy to get out of, or into. Our credentials were checked at a lodge between two walls, in each of which doors had to be unlocked by a blue-uniformed warder, who then saluted my uncle. We came out in a large courtyard, within which stood several elderly three-story brick cell blocks, a small greenhouse, a chapel, and a wood-framed administrative building, built in 1799, and topped with a cupola. All round, the high prison wall impeded a view of the world without. One was definitely "inside." Parkhurst is the prison most frequently used for the detention of long-term, serious offenders—you need at least a five-year sentence to go there—and it generally houses five hundred prisoners, for whom there is a prison staff of four hundred. Within Parkhurst, a prison inside a prison, is a maximum-security section which at this time had seventeen men in it, including some of those responsible for the Great Train Robbery.

"Our job is to detain prisoners with the least possible damage to their physical and mental health," said the six-foot-six Deputy Governor, Colin Heald, as he accompanied my uncle on his rounds. Mr. Heald kept a big bunch of keys in hand, for each doorway is double. Following the air-lock principle, used for getting out of a sunken submarine, the inner door has to be locked before the outer one is unlocked. Mr. Heald said, "We change the locks and keys pretty regularly—they're making keys all the time." But at each doorway, too, there seemed to be a prison officer, unarmed except with a truncheon, standing watch, ready to salute Mr. Heald and my uncle and turn the locks for them.

The cell halls emphasize the physical fact of Parkhurst—the rather melancholy fact that the buildings themselves determine far more than any idea or ideals of prison management what a prison is. One of the halls we looked into was three stories high, with galleries at each level and a net strung across the lower opening. "The net is not to prevent suicides," said Mr. Heald. "It's to protect the officers from objects bring dropped on them. But one man jumped last month—he thought the net would be a trampoline. He's still in hospital with a broken leg." We entered a cell, eight by twelve, with a single cot neatly made up, a small table and chair, a little window, a civilian shirt carefully hung over the back of the chair, and on the wall a glossy studio print of a good-looking girl, inscribed "Darling, with my love always."

The dungeon-like effect of the cell was somewhat re-
lieved by bright paint, and the cell was warm. Mr.
Heald said one of the few good things about the anti-
quated buildings was the Victorian hot-air central heating system, which—now converted from coal to oil—
functioned well.

We dodged a shower by ducking into the library next—
worn brown lino on the floor, yellowy varnished wood-
work, some twenty thousand books, mostly junk, but a
few good ones, newspapers, and magazines. I noted a
well-thumbed, ten-year-old copy of *Yachting World* that
had been bound. Several tanks of tropical fish. A kettle,
on a gas ring, was on the boil, and the teapot was standing ready. In nearby "association rooms," Spartanly
furnished, the men can meet for an hour or so every
night. Some study and learn languages; some watch TV.
Free films are shown once a month and for a small
weekly subscription the prisoners can belong to a film
club, which hires others.

My uncle had a few words with the chef when we
reached the kitchen. "One lot in one mess hall complained of too much flour in their soup last week," he
said. "But it turned out they'd refused to put up a man
for the food committee, and were just grumblers. The
food is usually all right." The hood over the ovens had
been painted with Neapolitan stripes. Stainless-steel vats
cooked five hundred portions. The chef said to my uncle,
"They're having cottage pie for lunch, sir, potatoes and
carrots. Then steamed pudding and tea. Egg and bacon
for supper." On trays ready for the oven were laid out
row on row of currant buns, about six inches in diameter,
the biggest I've ever seen. Anyone who needs a special
diet gets it. Food is important in Parkhurst, and in each

cell hall the day's menu is chalked up on a blackboard by the door.

There were fifty men in the prison hospital, ten from other prisons. We saw the radiological department, with brand-new machines. We saw the prisoner who had jumped on the gallery net. We saw seven men waiting to see the psychotherapist, and five waiting to see the dentist. We saw a young inmate helping an old man shuffle along with two canes and a bemused look on his face. "He's getting out next year," said my uncle. "But God knows where he'll go." The chapel, interdenominational, had a neither-one-thing-nor-the-other air: the pews were interdenominational oak, the glass interdenominationally colorless. "Attendance," said Mr. Heald, "is pretty poor." We walked past the heavily guarded gate of the maximum-security section. Two television cameras were trained on the doorway. The small recreation pitch was muddy, sloping. "The prison football team always wins its home games," said my uncle, wryly.

Apart from a few men in blue overalls helping in the kitchen, library, and grounds, we had seen no prisoners yet. They were in the workshops: a tinsmith's, where pots, pans, and cans were being made; and a tailor's shop, where clothes and aprons were being mass-produced. Parkhurst got rid of mailbag sewing several years ago, but Mr. Heald said this demeaning occupation had crept back in for the maximum-security prisoners, because other facilities were lacking. He thought several of the men in fact were brilliantly inventive, and their genius could be made profitable for themselves and society by giving them difficult research work. Work, at any rate, was Parkhurst's present problem. Under a so-called rationalization scheme affecting all British prisons, whereby each prison would specialize in one trade, Parkhurst was going to have to give up its tinsmith's shop and concentrate on tailoring. The prison staff thought it would be better to get rationalized into a system where Parkhurst men (who had often been convicted of violent crimes) had a more physically consuming task than needlework. The powers in the Home Office in London worried about security, it seemed, when considering these matters, but both my uncle and Mr. Heald seemed to think they worried unnecessarily. "A man can make a dagger if he wants to in any circumstances," said Mr. Heald. "But if he wants an offensive weapon he doesn't need to go to that extreme. A comb properly held or a boot properly wielded are weapons enough."

The men at the sewing machines and pattern-cutting tables had pale, indoor looks. Some glanced sidelong at the visitors, but most continued to snip at the patterns and push the cloth through the chattering needles of the machines, abstracted, caught up in a five- or twenty-year stretch of daydreams gathered around the single subject: getting out. Seeing them, a visitor unused to prisons finds himself fogged with pity. It is difficult to keep in mind the uncomfortable facts that these men, guests of Her Majesty at the cost of nearly three thousand dollars a year, have coshed old ladies, blown up banks, or proved otherwise unfriendly to the society that has put them here, where their marriages are cracking up, their children forgetting them. Mr. Heald and his men seemed to have developed an attitude of stern-cored good humor, like that of teachers in a tough school; but there were few graduations and scholarships. "We just hold on to them," Mr. Heald said, with a touch of exasperation. "We aren't effecting many cures."

The Isle of Wight!

Back in Mr. Heald's office, drinking tea, I read a copy of the bimonthly Parkhurst magazine, *Outlet*. (Prison magazines favor that sort of name, to judge from sister publications mentioned in *Outlet*. There is *Time*, of Joliet; *Penorama*, Quebec; and *Inside World*, Mississippi.) *Outlet* contains a stamp column, crossword, sexy pinup line drawings, short stories, a navigation primer (for crossing the Solent?), a satirical fashion column, film reviews (*The Great Escape*), a financial report with stock tips, an intelligent editorial page, sports columns, poems, and epigraphs sprinkled here and there from Darwin, Macaulay, and one Murphy, who apparently said, "The people of England are never so happy as when you tell them they are ruined." I liked the verse of Charles Baron Bowen (1835–94):

> *The rain it raineth on the just*
> *And also on the unjust fella,*
> *But chiefly on the just, because*
> *The unjust steals the just's umbrella.*

"And you should look at these," said Mr. Heald, bringing two leather-bound ledgers from a cupboard.

"Parkhurst was a boys' prison in the mid-nineteenth century," said my uncle. "Those were the entry books."

I turned over a few pages filled with fine copperplate handwriting. I stopped at random. In 1848, James Fraser, silk weaver, aged fourteen, whose offense was stealing rags (his first offense), was sentenced to seven years' transportation and embarked upon the ship *Joseph Somes* for Port Phillip. On other pages the names differed and the offense was sometimes stealing a loaf or a sixpence. The sentences were similar. Mr. Heald was discussing some matters my uncle intended to raise in a visit to the

Home Office the following week, and seeing that I had put the ledgers down, they paused for a moment and then, with no discourtesy, went on talking, refraining from underlining the conclusion I had come to, that, although things might not be right, at least they were better.

The weather cleared in the late afternoon. My father proposed a walk from Godshill, a few miles in from Shanklin, to Appuldurcombe, where my grandfather used to rent pasture for his herd and my father had come daily for the milk. "We used to bring the dairy horse out here for holidays," my father said, breaking the companionable silence in which we walked along past farms and through lush meadows. "But she didn't like it. After a day or so, we'd find her standing outside the shop in Shanklin. She walked back by herself." Our path brought us to the Freemantle Gate of Appuldurcombe Park, a stone central arch for carriages flanked by two smaller pedestrian archways and iron gates painted blue and yellow. The formality prepared one for more than there was: somewhat unkempt parkland, a lodge where we paid five pence, and then Appuldurcombe House, which, declares the sagacious Pevsner, "does not make as good a ruin as one might hope to find."

The house, an early-eighteenth-century mansion built of gray ashlar stone, is hollow now, with neither roof nor windows, and grass growing where floors had been. It was designed, Pevsner suggests, by "a minor provincial architect whose one great chance this was." Begun for Sir Robert Worsley, it was finished for Sir Richard Worsley, who collected Levantine antiquities and was the author of a history of the Isle of Wight. He wrote (1781) regarding Appuldurcombe, "The soil is very

rich, and affords excellent pasturage; beeches of uncommon magnitude, interspersed with venerable oaks,
form the back-ground above the house." It was occupied
by a college, then a monastery, and abandoned in 1901.
The gardens, designed by Capability Brown, are now
well tended by government gardeners, and my father—
who as a tourist at the White House in Washington
some years ago told a curator that the lawn there was in
dreadful shape—approved of the thick green clipped turf
growing here. There were still beeches and oaks, and
also holly, azaleas, and a yew with tortured outstretched
branches.

Back in Godshill, a village almost perilously quaint,
we found it was just opening time at the Griffin, a
double-fronted early-Victorian pub with gingerbread
(or what is here called bargeboarded) gables.

"It's been better this afternoon, hasn't it?" said the
red-haired bargeboarded lady behind the saloon bar,
drawing us two pints of Burts Special Bitter.

"Yes," we said.

"Good for this time of year, anyway."

"Looked like more rain, but it held off," said my
father.

"Sensible, I think, taking a holiday at this time of
year. You can't move through this place in July and
August."

"I suppose not."

"Coaches," said the lady. "Thick with coaches. They
come for the teas, and the thatch, of course. Stop here
and in the cafés. I pity them when it rains."

"Yes."

"Last August was dreadful, wasn't it?"

"It was pretty bad."

"But September picked up a little."

"Yes. The last two weeks . . ."

"And last month, sunshine every day. Same again? Just a half this time. Right you are."

Sunshine is important to British coastal resorts. Their daily sunshine record is published in the newspapers, and the yearly champion advertises success. Cleethorpes, in north Lincolnshire, has had such a bad record that there has been talk of installing infrared and ultraviolet lamps along its promenade. The Isle of Wight resorts are generally in the top few, and on the way back to the Savoy my father and I called in to see the local expert on the subject, Mr. Horace Hoare, who lives in a top-floor flat in Shanklin. Since retiring from running a brewery in 1944, he has been the town's meteorological observer.

"It's not everybody's pigeon," said Mr. Hoare, pouring us each a glass of homemade Curaçao. (Having given up the commercial production of beer, he has been making his own wine and liqueurs.) "It takes a good bit of time. I send a telegram in code to the Met Office at 1800 hours daily. I take the readings on my roof with a Campbell sunshine recorder—it's their standard model. A sunsphere, with slightly sensitized photographic paper, which smolders when the sun is out, gives you a record accurate down to the minute. I change the paper every night. Now, what about switching to this raspberry wine and seeing what you think of it?"

My father and I held out our glasses.

"The newspapers publish the Met Office figures," Mr. Hoare went on. "The figures are also useful in insurance cases. Someone claiming for frost damage to his crops, for example, is liable to have his claim checked against Met Office records. I don't have any instruments for thunder or wind. I make my own estimate. Last year, I was nearly blown off the roof—I estimated it at Force 10. It's also strange how different the weather can be between here and Sandown, two miles away. Once I recorded 6.9 hours of sunshine. Next day, they called me up from Sandown. They hadn't had any sun—not a blemish on their recording paper all day. They were furious, wouldn't believe me. I told them what I'd seen— a belt of fog running all the way from Keats Green to Culver Cliff, covering them. But these houses on Shanklin cliff had their top stories poking through the fog. Most bizarre."

My father congratulated Mr. Hoare on his wine-making ability.

"Ah, but you must try the parsnip. Most people don't realize you can make wine of anything. Sugar makes the wine, the rest is flavoring. In its first year, parsnip wine tastes like old rats, but when you've kept it awhile it's pretty good. Just after the last war, when a fair bottle of wine sold for thirty shillings, old Yelf, Sandown wine-and-spirits merchant, called on me. He was something of a wine taster. I got out the snifters and poured him some parsnip, saying it was unlabeled, couldn't tell what it was. He liked it. He said it was one of the finest Moselles he'd tasted, and he'd take two hundred bottles at a guinea apiece."

After dinner at the Savoy, my father and I decided not to mix our drinks, and since the pints of bitter at the Griffin were now a fading memory, this indicated a visit to the Wine Lodge, an establishment recently opened in the cellars of Mr. Hoare's former brewery. Shanklin, according to my Uncle Jim, who joined us there, is now quite lively out of season. Part of this is due to the island's growing retired population: one person in four is retired, a fact that annoys some natives who think the increased proportion of elderly people will have a baleful effect on island life. In fact, Shanklin now has three casinos operating year round, helping to assuage the desperate gambling ardor of the islanders, which is not otherwise sated by bookmakers' shops, football pools, and the ubiquitous slot machines. The one-arm bandit at the Savoy treated me kindly in the two days I was head-quartered there; my winnings were ninety pence. The headwaitress said that over five months, with a daily investment of fifty pence, she had won eighty pounds— a profit of five pounds. My father had an obligatory go on the one-arm bandit at the Wine Lodge, "just to see what turns up." He lost thirty pence before stopping. At the bar was a dapper young man, complaining of just having had breakfast, whom my uncle recognized as a croupier from one of the casinos. Customs and excise figures indicate that the British gamble more than two and a half billion pounds a year. In any event, on the island the hot pace of modern life is not whole-heartedly welcome. "Overners"—trippers, visitors, and immigrants from the mainland—bring vitality and cash, but they are also doing away with the slow season, when islanders had room and time to chat with friends and bother less about their businesses. Island bus fares are still lower in the off-season, but other distinctions—like lots of free parking space—are fast fading. My uncle said the Shanklin cobbler had complained to him recently that he was down on the beach at midnight, casting in the surf, when suddenly a car drew up on the promenade and a man came running down the beach, waving a pair of shoes: "Thought I'd find you here," he said. "Soles and heels as soon as you can do them."

When my father and uncle get together, I sometimes

find out a little about my recent ancestors. My knowledge of them is slight, based as it is on chance remarks and childhood suggestions. Until this evening, I had believed my grandfather had run away from home to be a cowboy in Montana, but now, asked about it, my father and uncle denied the tale. "Montana? Where's that? No, he was in Virginia, farming for a few years. He brought back a big Western saddle. That may have made you think of cowboys. And he didn't run away. His father sent him." But I had got them going, and my father described how my grandfather used to sit at night in the cellar of the Shanklin dairy, testing eggs by holding them in front of a candle. Now and then, the milk was made to go a bit further on rainy days by leaving the lids off the churns for a while before bringing them in. "He had barrels of beer in the cellar, Jim, do you remember?" said my father. "He used to send me down to draw off a pint for him."

"Now our grandfather, *your* great-grandfather, was the boy," my uncle said to me. "He was the founder of the firm. He was a director of Shanklin Pier and Daish's Hotel. He had thirteen children, a lot of them girls, who turned out to be maiden aunts, and he didn't leave much by the time he'd set them up for the rest of their lives."

I had a late start next morning from Ventnor, and not too clear a head. I walked out through Bonchurch, a rock garden of a village, and paused in St. Boniface churchyard to look at Swinburne's grave. It is in the family plot, on the path to the church door, with an admiral for a neighbor on one side and four other Swinburnes on the other. The simple stone gives the name, Algernon Charles Swinburne, and the dates April 5, 1837, April 10, 1909. Thomas Hardy came here and wrote a poem,

"A Singer Asleep." Time is dense here, and even the road, called Bonchurch Shute, is deep between banks and hedges, like a river worn into the ground. I went down it toward the shore, past Bonchurch Old Church, which was rebuilt (according to a sign) in 1070.

Perhaps a hangover isn't a bad condition for taking— as one does in this Ventnor–Shanklin section—so strong a dose of the picturesque. Olmsted saw more or less the same sights one hundred and twenty-five years ago: "Dark . . . rugged ravines, chasms and watergaps, grand rocks, and soft, warm, smiling, inviting dells and dingles; and, withal, there is a strange and fascinating enrichment of foliage, more deep, graceful and luxuriant, than I ever saw before." The path crosses the Landslip, a collapse of part of the shoreline which occurred in 1818— large rocks, dense vegetation, and signposted paths on which this morning there were quite a few people walking: two lady hikers with stout sticks, an elderly couple, and a young man and his miniskirted girl. An early-nineteenth-century *Guide to British Watering Places* declared that the Isle of Wight's young females had "a loveliness of form, and beauty of countenance, not to be found so generally in any other district of Britain." I think the writer of that would say the same today.

I went through Shanklin at a good clip, past the Savoy and Bailey's, past private hotels with names like Sandringham and Manor Lodge, past the tumbled gardens of the Chine, and past the thatch and bargeboards of the few cottages left from the Shanklin of Keats's time. When Keats first saw the village, he liked the clefts and sloping woods and "the sea, Jack, the sea—the little waterfall—then the white cliff." In 1819, here a second time, writing "Lamia" and revising "Hyperion," he wasn't well and the town was full of tourists, prowling with spyglasses in search of the picturesque—"like beagles," said Keats. As for himself, "I may call myself an old Stager in the picturesque, and unless it be something very large and overpowering I cannot receive any extraordinary relish."

The tide was out. I walked along the beach from Shanklin to Sandown. In a way, this was cheating, for Shanklin, Sandown, and the intervening village of Lake have become the conurbation of the Isle of Wight— hardly a spread city but a spread seaside town. But I am an old Stager in megalopolises, and on the beach, under the red cliffs, I avoided the interminable brick villas and stucco boarding houses, and made do with the tide pools, the smell of seaweed, and the graffiti with which past visitors had attempted to immortalize their holiday preoccupations. (In one spot on the cliffs, someone had carved PAT IS LOOKING FOR A GIRL and in another, MANCHESTER UNITED.) I stopped, however, at the boathouse of Mr. Ivan Hooper, my uncle's father-in-law. Mr. Hooper, who had recently celebrated his eighty-second birthday, used to *row* the morning catch of local fish from Sandown to Southsea—a round trip of twenty-five miles. I found him varnishing the seats of a stout, clinker pulling-boat, of the kind he rents to summer visitors. "You're just in time," he said. "The cliff and beach are washing away. Won't be here long, the way they are setting about it." I gathered "they" were the local council, and they were planning to build groins, which are stout wooden walls made of pilings driven into the sand and running out at right angles to the line of the shore. Mr. Hooper didn't think the groins would preserve the cliff, which stands here over a level of blue slipper clay. Mr. Hooper thought, instead, shallow embankments should be built at the head of the beach to spend the force of the water, "like turning a sheep over on its back." He added, "I never mind a wave as long as it's white—then you know it's got air in it. It's those big black buggers I don't like."

The sand is a medium tan, the perfect consistency for castles, harbors, embankments, and islands—the geography of childhood. On this beach I paddled, buried myself to the neck in sand, played and warred with other children, got lost, and won first prize in the under-eight division of a fancy-dress competition as Tarzan, wearing a piece of imitation leopard skin. The competition took place on Sandown Pier, which time had shrunk. It was smaller, less fantastic than I'd remembered, with no sideshows, amusement arcades, bingo parlors, or crazy house with sloping floors and distorting mirrors. At Blackgang Chine, there is a curiosity museum inside the skeleton of a whale—the sort of thing that belongs on a pier, together with penny-in-the-slot machines showing "What the Butler Saw," and postcards of comic and scatological intent. The seaside is a place where the British change into bathing suits with a lot of wriggling and grunting under towels, and the humorous possibilities are threadbare and infinite. It was memory and other places that had added to Sandown Pier for me. I walked out over its weathered planking, between whose cracks one could see the sea rising and falling like a concertina. Two lady anglers spoke to each other as I passed. It was as if they exchanged ten words once an hour:

"I think I'll shorten mine up a bit now."

"I've just let mine out a little."

I had half a pint of Double Diamond draft bitter, two Scotch eggs, a cold sausage, tomatoes, and some pickled onions in the Islander bar, on the pier head, and then walked up the curving, hilly streets. In summer, Sandown shops sold (and still sell) sand shoes and sneakers (called plimsolls), buckets and spades, inflatable beach toys, ice cream, and rock, which is the British equivalent of saltwater taffy—a hard, cylindrical piece of peppermint candy with the name of the particular resort running through it in section, as it were. All the way through, as you lick or bite, there is SANDOWN in a fuzzy, sticky glow before you. I stopped from pure nostalgia in front of one confectioner's small shop window and noted the ranks of tall glass jars on the shelves—butter Brazils, acid-drop thins, mint scotch, acid drops, mint bonbons, sherbet fruits, chocolate dragons, butter mints, kop kopps, butterscotch, assorted butters, chocolate-éclair candies, glacier mints, mint lumps, old-fashioned humbugs, chocolate toffees, clear mints, fruit drops, Brazil patties, licorice all-sorts, almond crescents, and barley sugars, not to mention innumerable brands and types of chocolate and indescribable cheap confections for children. Some people have a sweet tooth, but the British have sweet teeth.

I also paused to look at Netherwood, my grandparents' former house on Station Avenue. I had remembered it as a large, wide-fronted gray stone house, with a sweeping veranda on which my grandfather used to sit in a wicker armchair. But what it was was a narrow semi-detached house, built of brick, with a pretty skimpy porch—though it had a conservatory at the side and stretched back a long way in the rear.

North of Sandown, the going was flat for a while: miniature golf course, artificial boating pond, mediocre landscaping, banal architecture—no taste, no gusto, no authentic vulgarity. It was a relief to reach rising ground behind Yaverland. The cliff climbs, too—first red, then white at Culver, the most easterly of the island chalk. Culver Cliff is 254 feet high and a constant challenge to island youth. My father and my uncle climbed it as young men. So did Swinburne, testing his own courage after his father refused to let him join the army. He climbed it twice, in fact, the second time immediately after his first attempt had been balked a foot or so from the top by an awkward overhang. I think it changes one's notion of him, built up as that notion popularly is of alliteration, angst, and alcoholism. For myself, I stayed on the path, a few feet from the cliff edge. From the top, there is a fine view south over Sandown Bay and a view eastward of rusty barbed wire, a rusty water tank, and a row of damn-your-eyes semi-detached cottages, presumably put up either to camouflage, or to house the crew of, the big naval guns that were here between the wars, guarding the approaches to Spithead and the Portsmouth navy yard. There is also a monument—but then few Isle of Wight down summits seem to lack them. This short stone obelisk is dedicated to Charles Anderson Pelham, Earl of Yarborough, Baron Worsley of Appuldurcombe, First Commodore of the Royal Yacht Squadron. The inscription goes on, "As the owner of large estates, he was one of those most conspicuous for the qualities which particularly adorn that station." This ponderous circumlocution seemed to leave enough room between the lines in which to read things. At any rate, the memorialist decided some detail was needed, and added that the noble earl helped improve the naval architecture and advanced the maritime interests of his country, and died (as any yachtsman would be happy to die) aboard his yacht *Kestrel*, at Vigo, Spain, aged sixty-five.

I slithered down the north side of Culver on a clay path

wet from the rain the day before. I slid past a woman who said, sympathetically, as I went by out of control, that she wished she'd worn her "hikers." My hikers had rubber soles worn smooth. But I kept my balance, and slowed down to a diplomatic pace as I crossed a field at the bottom, occupied by a hefty-shouldered brown bull. I hunched my shoulders, too, the idea being to conceal the collar of my red L. L. Bean flannel shirt. Were my ears red? I made it across his domain and climbed, with no wasted movement, the stile on the far side of the field.

Bembridge, St. Helens, Seaview, Ryde: the last eight miles. In Bembridge, a refined village, children were just coming out of school and I bought a choc-ice from an ice-cream vendor who had planted himself strategically at the one pedestrian street crossing. The road to St. Helens, alongside Brading Harbor, belongs to British Railways and a sign details tolls for trucks, cars, and horses. "Charge for pedestrians, one penny."

I said to the elderly toll-keeper, "Charge for pedestrians?"

"We're supposed to, sir, but we don't."

"Thank you very much."

"Not a bit, sir. Good afternoon."

Brading Harbor at low tide is a muddy creek, lined with houseboats—old patrol boats, fishing boats, cabin cruisers, and wartime floating bridge pontoons with all-year-round bungalow superstructures. Struts and posts hold the slimmer craft upright in their mud berths. Stove pipes come out at odd angles; decks are covered with tar paper; one boat had a letter box where its anchor hawse pipe might once have been. At the head of the harbor, where the smell of the gasworks was strong, two swans and three pearl-gray cygnets cruised in the fresher waters of the eastern Yar. Thus through St. Helens, a pleasant and unpretentious village set round a long village green, across a muddy field and past a holiday camp, and through the wet woods behind Node's Point, where a building called the Priory, the property of the Workers' Travel Association, is surrounded in the best landowning spirit by signs indicating precisely what is and what is not a public right-of-way. Here, as in other parts of the island, a lane private for vehicles may be public for walkers. Exercising my prerogative as a pedestrian, I got down to the water at Seaview, a tidy little town whose prospect is of Spithead rather than of the open sea, and includes the dour forts planted in the shallows in Palmerston's time to guard its entrance. The French under Napoleon III were the enemies in a cold war then.

Off Ryde East Sands, the tide goes out a long way—the submarine *Alliance* had through faulty navigation run aground there the week before. I walked along the shorefront promenade, with its stone railings and sheltered seats, past Puckpool Point and St. John's Park, and into Ryde. From a distance, I could see my father standing, beyond the Hovercraft terminus, at the entrance to Ryde Pier, at the far end of which the ferryboat to the mainland was waiting. "We're in no hurry, are we?" he said, over the racketing noise of a Hovercraft coming in. "How about going the old way?"

I agreed.

MEMORIES OF

A DAY'S WALK FROM

MASSACHUSETTS

TO MAINE

IN THE EVENING, hitchhiking back, I was quickly faced with the question of what I was doing there, a mile or so out of New Castle, New Hampshire, thumb pointing south, one foot supported by a yellow fire hydrant improbably stuck by the dusty rural roadside, and my green nylon knapsack propped where the late-in-the-day, late-August light might dwell on it as evidence of an honest traveler. But since with strangers, even those kind enough to give one a ride, one has the right to shorten one's explanations, I said simply, "I've just walked the New Hampshire coastline." There was also the fact that, just then, starting back down a road I had trudged along a few hours before, I felt enveloped in a sort of concentricity, with time curled up on itself, my mind warm and swollen and in a blurry tingle, like my feet—I must have walked some twenty-two miles, counting the ins and outs and a few reverses—and I didn't feel like enlarging on my reasons why. There were various answers, or parts of answers, anyway, to questions of motive. I could borrow Mallory's response "Because it is there"—in New Hampshire's case not record height like Everest, but record brevity, the coast being eighteen

miles long as a seagull might fly it, the shortest coastline
of any state touching salt water; or I could give another
answer, that I was born on the coast of old Hampshire,
England, but now lived mostly in London and took whatever chance I could of walking in sight of the sea. Or I
could say that I was visiting old friends who, since I'd
seen them last, had separated. I had a day free between
seeing them separately, one in one Massachusetts town,
one in another. An appropriate time, and time enough,
to go walking.

I set off northward along the New Hampshire beach
at 7:50 a.m.—sand behind me, sand to my left, sand in
front, and to my right the calm sea: small wavelets
running in; sun low and very bright; a barely perceptible
offshore breeze to be felt on my left ear. I had left my
car on Route 1A, two hundred yards inland over the
slight ridge of dunes, where the honky-tonk sprawl of
Salisbury Beach, the last town in Massachusetts, petered
out at a road junction with a few cottages, gas station,
traffic lights, and restaurant signs. Just north of the junction, a big road sign said "Welcome to / *Bienvenue au*
New Hampshire." I failed to rouse any response in the
house attached to a narrow roadside lot where all-day
parking was advertised for one dollar (and offenders who
failed to pay were threatened with being towed away). I
walked, therefore, across 1A to a combination gas station
and general store called Salisbury Building Supply
(which also sold Frisbees, fishing gear, and newspapers).
A mustachioed young man who stood behind the till
took the dollar bill I proffered as a parking fee and
handed me fifty cents. I asked him if he could tell me
exactly where New Hampshire began. He said, "Out
through the door, about four yards on your left." I parked
my old Saab on what was as yet the shady side of the

building, front wheels in Massachusetts, back wheels in New Hampshire. So far, the day was cloudless. I left my raincoat and shoes in the car, donning an elderly white cricket sweater, worn blue sailing sneakers, and a broad-brimmed olive-green ex–British Army bush hat—an item military historians might take into account when pondering Britain's success (compared with other nations conducting counter-insurgency operations) in quelling terrorists in the Malayan jungles. Wallet, spare socks, notebook, Texaco road map, geological survey map, and Coastal Chart 1206 (Portsmouth to Cape Ann) went into the knapsack. I popped back into the store to ask the man whether there was any public transport back down the coast I intended to walk—any trains, buses?

"Nope—not a thing."

"Then I guess I'll have to hitchhike back."

"Yep. Nothing like the good old thumb."

On the beach, I fell into an optimistic northbound stride. The low light, sweeping in from the sea over the gently tilted expanse of sand, gave dramatic prominence to the people already there: four solitary joggers; a man slowly searching the beach with a metal detector, caressing it almost, as if polishing a floor; several dog owners being taken for exercise by their pets; and, in two ragged ranks to one side of the gap in the dunes through which I'd come, what in that light might have have been taken for the larvae of a giant insect—long brown and green tubes which wriggled, opened, and released forms that stood up, stretched, yawned, and sometimes hugged one another. As I went by, one pair of teenagers who had spent the summer night thus in their sleeping bags ran to the water's edge and stuck their feet in an in-running wavelet and, to judge by their squeals, found it chilly.

The air, too, had a go-fast nip to it. The tide was roughly half up, and I walked midway between the water's edge and the high-tide line, following a strip of flat, hard, gravelly sand. On it, the footprints of joggers could be recognized by an abrupt ridge of pushed-back sand—the aft end of the mark made by the ball of a foot. There were also footprints of dogs, the trident marks of gulls' feet in the darker sand beside the tide pools, and— farther up the beach—the rippled tire tracks of a six-wheeled former army truck onto which debris from litter drums was being emptied. The sand was furrowed in some places into miniature ravines and deltas, where water ran off seaward. The asphalt-shingled roofs of modest summer bungalows peered over the fringe of dunes; the roofs thickened not far ahead into the community—municipally complete with water tower and at least two Stars and Stripes on flagstaffs—of Seabrook Beach. Beyond, the visible coast stretched northward as far as a promontory I identified on the chart as Great Boars Head, roughly four miles distant. Seaward, the horizon seemed higher than one expected: I felt as if I were walking in a valley banked with sand and water; both nearby rocks and far-off fishing boats sat high on the sea's surface. The onshore light, glinting off the sea, skipping off tide pools and sand and forming dark caves and slots under the cottage eaves and porches, had lost the hazy look of summer. It had an autumnal chiaroscuro, a specific New England property that is the effect of sunlight of a southern strength in a northern landscape. (Winslow Homer and Edward Hopper come to mind as painters who have captured it.) Meanwhile, my shadow, knapsacked and bush-hatted, progressed at right angles to me, uphill on my left.

At 8:25 I reached the first break in the coast—in fact, a breakwater composed of large granite blocks, forming the southern side of the entrance to Hampton Harbor, a marsh-backed estuary at the junction of the Hampton Falls River and Taylor River. Here, warmed up by now, I took off and stowed away my sweater. A party fishing boat, complete with party on deck, was bludgeoning its way out against the tide—whose incoming was announced by a black can buoy, C7, tilted inland. Less organized individuals, including a number of small boys, were already fishing off the end of the breakwater. To the northeast, offshore six miles or so, could be made out the silhouetted humps and whalebacks of the Isles of Shoals; from that angle, which placed some islands in front of others, there appeared to be only two of them, rather than seven. Westward up the harbor entrance lay the bridge that carries Route 1A, the only way across the channel. But when I started toward it I ran up against a barrier of private gardens and fences belonging to a prosperous clump of houses at this corner of beach. Evidently, a lot of people were put in a similar quandary here, for in the otherwise inviting yard of a modern gray-cedar house stood a sign: "Exit to road 7 houses back." I therefore went back and found between two houses a sandy path lined with chain-link fencing, leading to the quiet streets of what might have been a year-round subdivision, unromantic except for the many Italian and French names outside the houses. At the Jolivets', an additional sign proclaimed that metal detectors could be bought within (I assume all the loose change that falls out of the pockets and purses of beach-goers is the lure.) Not a person was to be seen in the streets, though numerous cabbage butterflies were taking an 8:35 spin. The houses were eerily quiet. In one front yard, a pale woman in her late forties lay sleeping in an aluminum garden chair. Had she spent the night there? I'd gone past when the name Cedarburg jumped into my head. I spent a long summer college vacation in Wisconsin, and one of several jobs I had for sustenance and pocket money was assembling garden loungers. Several days a week, I came in from my digs in the outlying town of Cedarburg to work for a sweet couple called the Jungs. They lived in a pastoral suburb of Milwaukee with an apple orchard, a garden store, and a lissome seventeen-year-old daughter named Susie. I picked apples, read Yeats and MacNeice to Susie, chatted to the Jungs over lunch about the wild doings of Senator Joseph McCarthy, and in the afternoons bolted together the webbing-covered tubular frames that formed the light, stretched-open Z shape of the loungers. (I believe I still could—if handed the cardboard box in which the parts came—assemble one in three minutes, possibly while declaiming MacNeice's "The sunlight in the garden, / Hardens and grows cold, / We cannot cage the minute / Within its nets of gold. / When all is told / We cannot beg for pardon.") At summer's end, I hitchhiked to New York to get the boat back to England. Come to think of it, that, twenty-odd years ago, was my last serious venture in free road travel.

New Hampshire (1938), the WPA guide to the state, says that in 1657 a stone on the dunes near Hampton Harbor entrance was inscribed to mark the then boundary between Massachusetts and New Hampshire, but I didn't see it. In 1938, the bridge here was wooden and cars had to pay a fifteen-cent toll to make the crossing. Now it is steel, and free, with a bascule section that lifts for boats needing the headroom. I walked across it a few yards behind a barefoot girl in flared blue jeans. Perhaps we should note for future historians that some in our time went barefoot by choice or from fashion, and not out of necessity.

Hampton Beach is the town on the north side of the span. It is also well placed at the seaward end of Route 101, a multi-lane highway that comes in at right angles to the shore from Manchester and other inland points and gives Hampton Beach good reason still for the WPA guide's description of it as "the mecca of hundreds of thousands of vacationists." Atlantic City rather than Mecca is the resort you would probably think of in Hampton Beach, though the scale of things is smaller. A wide, oceanfront boulevard aptly named Ocean Boulevard has amusement arcades, a state beach, and various hotels and motels with such names as Sea Breeze, Hollywood, Sea Den, Alecia, King Neptune, Blue Haven, and Sun 'n Surf. Suggestions are made that the Hampton Beach vacationing crowd is cosmopolitan—or at least French Canadian. *"Ici on parle français,"* a sign said outside one motel. *"Remorquage à vos frais,"* which means "Towed away at your expense," declared a placard in a private parking lot. Between the boulevard and the beach lay a long municipal parking area, with parking meters, and the green-and-white license plates of New Hampshire cars, each presenting the belligerent—but evidently rather wishful—state motto, "Live Free or Die."

At 9 a.m., Hampton Beach had the feeling of bustle building up: kids were arriving on the sand and getting their kites off the ground, flicking Frisbees, and laying the foundations for sand sculptures; bike and beach-umbrella rental stands were being opened for the day; elderly couples were parking their cars and getting out for a short stroll, quite a few of them speaking French.

Other cars were moving remarkably slowly along the boulevard—partly perhaps because of the holiday atmosphere, partly because of frequent 10 m.p.h. speed-limit signs and cruising police cars. Drivers were politely yielding to cars parking or unparking, and were stopping to allow pedestrians to cross the roadway. I walked along the seafront promenade, noting but refusing to be ensnared by the restaurants and cafés on the other side of the boulevard. Advertisements begged passersby to sample their breakfast specials—"fried dough" being one that intrigued me, though not, then and there, to the point of actually wanting to sit down in front of a plate of it. (Other Hampton Beach fare, presumably for later in the day, included a bucket of spaghetti and eight meatballs for $4.50.) I took in the fact that the Bavarian Brauhaus Band was scheduled to play in the Sea Shell Stage from 7 to 8:30 p.m., while from a free copy of *Beach News*, picked up in the information booth next to the auditorium, I learned that the big movies showing on the shore that week were *Tidal Wave* and *Jaws*. I stored away the information that at 7 p.m. daily the Seabrook Greyhound bus left the Ashworth Hotel for the Seabrook dog track, offering, if all else failed, a possible partway trip back to my car. On Friday, the local Chamber of Commerce intended to "host" the weekly New Hampshire Sweeps drawing at the Sea Shell, with beach towels being awarded courtesy of the New Hampshire Sweepstakes Commission. Lotteries and sweepstakes have a long and useful past in no-state-tax New Hampshire: one institution that was given a boost by them is Dartmouth College.

Indeed, New Hampshire seems to have concluded some time back that man's baser instincts might as well be put to public use: not only betting but drinking, with grog shops run by the state government, and liquor sold comparatively cheap. But to make up for this largesse, numerous signs along the shore prohibit the consumption of alcoholic drinks on state beaches. And, perhaps to make up for *that*, other activities the Puritans might have frowned on were being countenanced as I walked through Hampton Beach: on the sand just past the Sea Shell Stage, I saw five swimsuited girls in a neat circle playing gin rummy; nearby, a boy and a girl on a beach towel were having a morning cuddle.

Walking, and especially walking on beaches, provides good exercise for one's memory. I passed a green notice board with the chalked information that high tide that day was 11:12 a.m., low tide 5:05 p.m. The water temperature was yet to be announced. Another notice told the public to "Contact Life Guard About Lost Children." I remember being lost on the beach at Sandown, Isle of Wight, when I was four or five—or rather (the truth doesn't turn up until one begins thinking about the occasion more intently), remember being found, being hugged and kissed, "Nothing to worry about, it's all right," and recall how vast that tiny beach had seemed with nearly the whole population of the known world on it and no sign of my parents or my bucket and spade. And possibly because the water of the English Channel in those prewar British summers didn't strike me as hospitably warm, forcing me to take adventurous excursions on foot, I didn't learn to swim until I reached America the first time—was "evacuated" for the duration of the war in Europe, and found myself, with great good fortune, living with an Ohio family who spent the summer of 1941 on Cape Cod. In Chatham, aged eight, on the splendid beach which encloses Pleasant Bay, I discovered that the withdrawing tide left pools of various depths, which were soon heated by the sun. So I proceeded from shallow pool to deep, from feet on the bottom to strenuous dog paddle, and on Labor Day was awarded the cup for the dog-paddle stakes in the end-of-season swim meet of the local beach club. The cup still sits in a glass-fronted corner cupboard in my parents' house, my sole contribution of prize silverware among the many pieces won at county athletic meets by my father, a middle-distance runner.

I was forced to stay on Route 1A for the next mile or so, behind Great Boars Head and along North Beach. The beach, already narrow by natural circumstance, was made even more so by the rising tide. Rather than hop from rock to rock, I walked on the sidewalk, which was sheltered from the waves of storms by a four-foot-high green-painted steel seawall, a bit rusty in places. From this point, I could see the remainder of the New Hampshire coast stretching ahead—could see, in fact, across the mouth of the Piscataqua River, where the state ends, to Gerrish Island, Maine. From this angle, four of the Isles of Shoals were visible. At this point, too, it became palpable that my sailing sneakers weren't ideal road shoes, and at 10 a.m. I was happy to clamber down to the actual beach again. Here, at the north end of North Beach, groins had been built of large granite blocks to preserve the sand, and seemed to be doing their job. But the beach thus formed was zigzag, the seaward edge of the sand between each groin slanting outward toward the northeast. From dry sand on one side of a groin, one climbed over the granite barrier and was met with water on the other side. This forced one to scramble inland a little along the groin before arriving over dry beach again that one could jump down to. Inland, behind a single row of houses spaced out on the inshore side of 1A, marshy meadows ran for a mile or so westward; then there was a range of low green hills. Along the road itself, a procession of cars streamed north, faster here, perhaps, because under the seawall drivers had no view of the sea. Unlike cars that notoriously flood into cities on weekday mornings with a single occupant, these cars were generally full to bursting with children, dogs, sleeping bags, suitcases, and sometimes bikes on the back, carried like lifeboats in davits.

Here I began to wonder about 1A's potential for southbound hitchhikers. An unworthy thought at this time of the morning, no doubt. Would Scott have reached the South Pole if he'd worried about getting back? Ah, but Scott didn't get back. My hitchhiking life flashed before me. At one time or another, I had given plenty of rides to high-school students clearly stranded by later-than-usual school hours and no bus service, and to backpacking youngsters on the way from London to the cross-Channel ferries. But I'd also passed a lot of hitchhikers by in the years since I had last put myself out on that particular roadside limb, and I doubted if my standing was good in the record of whatever god or goddess (Mercury? Iris?) looked after hitchhikers' interests. Drivers, of course, think of the risks to them, but as I remember it, the peril for the rider should also be considered. One wet Good Friday, hitching from Dieppe to Paris, I was given a lift by a French angler, and drinker, who as the car went round the bends of a slippery *route nationale* at numerous kilometers an hour kept taking his hands off the steering wheel to demonstrate to me, in the back among his rods and baskets, the length of a fish he had caught or was going to catch (the tenses were hard to make out), often turning round to grin amiably at me as he gestured. Coming east from Wisconsin, armed with cardboard and crayon for making destination signs, I had an apprehensive ride across part of Indiana with a man whose business card, produced with a snap of the fingers from a point in midair up near the rearview mirror, proclaimed him a vice-president of the International Society of Magicians. (I expected rabbits to pop from the cigar lighter. I neglected to ask how the lady was sawn in half.) And from Chillicothe, Ohio, to Charleston, West Virginia, on the great-circle route I took to New York City, I rode with a truck driver whose reminiscences consisted largely of the number of times he had overturned his tractor-trailer rig, skidding great distances and skittling Burma-Shave signs.

At the north end of North Beach, a small, unnamed promontory gave a measure of shelter from the north and west to a dozen boats moored there, bobbing. Two lads were joyfully rowing a pair of brightly painted dories in the gentle surf. I made my way over the rocks that buttressed the headland, with its complement of unpretentious, well-built shingled summer houses. The rocks, interspersed with patches of mud and eel grass, ran out to an offshore ledge, and as I negotiated them, three small girls in swimsuits came by. One, also wearing purple bedroom slippers, said to her friends, "You guys going out on the rocks?" It was the sort of place where things are assembled by wind and tide. I saw a dead seagull; a single flip-flop; fragments of foam mattress; a crushed take-away coffee container; a plastic spoon; a frayed strand of polypropylene lobster-pot line. But very little driftwood. There were midges in the air, and a swooping band of swallows, presumably gobbling up midges. Friends had warned me of the possibility of "greenheads"—fearsome flies that torment beachgoers, at least in Massachusetts, forcing communities to set up expensive trap boxes to try to catch them. But so far no greenheads.

One difficulty with beach walking is that after a while you feel one leg is getting longer than the other. As I stepped out onto the sand again, I tried walking backward for a way to put things into balance. It may not have helped my muscles, but it certainly gave me more "visibility." Several people, turning their heads to look at me, said "Good morning," and an elderly man in sun hat, swimsuit, and sneakers called out, "How's it going there, young fella?" On the extensive porch of one beachfront house, a crowd of informally dressed people had gathered. I was wondering if it was a property owners' meeting, when I heard a boy call out to a woman coming down the steps from the porch, "Was he old?" Perhaps it was—albeit in bright Bermuda shorts and terry-towel wraps—a wake.

For a change, the parking lot at this North Hampton beach (just south of Little Boars Head) was free. However, one had to pay if one wanted to use the little shingled bathhouses—fifty cents for a quick change, $3.00 daily rate, according to a sign. I crossed 1A behind the beach at this point in order to reach the Sand Dollar Sandwich Shoppe for what back home we call elevenses. I'd had a boiled egg and an English muffin for breakfast much earlier that morning, and now felt the need of some small thing to get me through to lunchtime. I found a place at the crowded counter, next to a woman eating a blueberry muffin, which looked scrumptious. When approached by one of the pair of somewhat sullen-looking girls—who wore the nurse-like uniform of white dress and white shoes that is apparently *de rigueur* for summer help along this coast—I said I would like a cup of coffee and a blueberry muffin, please. "We're fresh out of blueberry muffins," she said. "How about an English?"

I'm usually a pushover for English muffins. I some-times take a large box of Thomas's back to England, since the English muffin as known in America is just about unobtainable there (Sainsbury's, a supermarket chain, sells a muffin that isn't a patch on Thomas's) and I've gone off a former love, the crumpet. But one muffin a day keeps desire at bay. I made do with a coffee while I tried to read that morning's Manchester (N.H.) *Union Leader* (a single-seat space at coffee shops doesn't give much scope for page turning; I read what I could of the *Union Leader*'s front page, folded up, on my lap). The paper goes in for blue headlines, a bouncy line in white stars on a blue band printed down the right-hand margin, and under the paper's name an epigraph from Daniel Webster: "There is nothing so powerful as truth." How-ever, this particular edition seemed to support the belief that there is nothing as effective as tickling the reader's sense of *déjà vu*. I was carried back to the summer of 1953 and McCarthy country by the banner headline, SOVIETS GET U.S. WARNING, subheaded "Told to Keep 'Hands Off' of Portugal." Surely a redundant "of"? The front-page editorial began flatly and ungrammatically "The key to straightening out the mess that this country is to be found is in informing the people of the United States as to what is actually going on." The woman on my left, who had just finished the ultimate blueberry muffin, was saying to her female companion, "But if they're not living together anymore, why does she still get up at seven?"

The southwest breeze had bestirred itself while I was in the Sand Dollar. The flap of my knapsack blew against the back of my neck and had to be secured before I walked on. Offshore, darker patches of wind-ruffled water seemed to travel seaward, where a gray lobster boat was hauling and shooting traps off Little Boars Head. The road climbed the headland, which, despite its name, is a good deal more impressive than Great Boars Head. Beside an introductory bend of the road, a gardener was weeding a big cambered bank of flowers, including phlox and chrysanthemums, provided by the local residents' association. The local residents didn't have their names on their gates or mailboxes, but according to the WPA guide, which in these dynastic matters may still have some force, "from the south and rounding the curve in the road appear in order the Studebaker estate, and the Nutting, Fuller, Spaulding, Manning, and Studebaker mansions." The mansions were what people in Newport call cottages—big, well-built 1920s houses with (one imagined) butler's pantries, nurseries, and laundry chutes. Garden contractors were at work on the spacious lawns, their pickup trucks parked in the driveways, their mowers mowing, and their hedge clippers buzzing. There was actually a sidewalk here, and a trim grass verge on the sea side of the road, which was now a corniche thirty or forty feet above the rocks. Bushes and plants had a placed look about them, and several comfortable varnished pine benches had been set there for people who wanted to sit and admire the view. The additional height above sea level allowed one to see the whole sweep of the coast southward round Ipswich Bay to the tip of Cape Ann. To the north, off Portsmouth, New Hampshire, and the mouth of the Piscataqua, a huge black tanker rode at anchor.

Little Boars Head merges with Fox Hill Point, and the coast then makes a shallow concave dip to the town of Rye Beach. There were neither boars nor foxes to be seen, but plenty of birds. Six cormorants and a lone black-backed gull stood on a single rock, half awash, while in the adjacent swell twenty-four ducks swam, riding high—exactly a dozen couples, or so it seemed, reinforcing my doubts about the natural rightness of the metric system. I also saw four plump but graceful downy gray birds, which later consultation with Roger Tory Peterson's guidebook led me to think were dowitchers or knots; a flock of sanderlings skittering along the water's edge; and, in a pond on the inland side of the road, a heron, standing so still I wondered if it was a statue of a heron, heron-still. Beach rose, beach plum, morning glory, bayberry, and goldenrod grew in niches and patches between the rocks. The sidewalk turned into a genuine boardwalk, on which I headed toward Rye Beach. Six-inch-wide planks, twelve to fifteen feet long, were laid four abreast on the summit of a man-made stone-and-shingle embankment protecting the road from the sea. The planks, clattering a little as I walked along them, made a pleasant change from sand and asphalt. Moreover, the contact with what's there, through the soles of one's feet, that one gets while walking produces a marvelous equanimity. Down below on the road, a yellow Corvette went snorting by, driven by a bare-chested youth who had one arm on the wheel, the other round the shoulders of his girl passenger. He shouted something up at me—words I didn't get, but the tone was arrogant and abusive. I threw him a cheerful, dismissive wave. (If I had been in a car he was overtaking, hearing him shout the same thing, I would have been furious.) On the narrow boardwalk I encountered only a ten-speed Peugeot, pedaled rapidly toward me by a boy in a bright-red T-shirt. I stepped aside onto the stones to let him pass and got a wave of thanks.

I kept up a good pace through Rye Beach—though tempted by a pizzeria, and sudden desire for a *quattro stagioni* of the kind I used to order at Luigino's on West Forty-eighth Street. (The pleasure of eating pizza at Luigino's was finally undermined by continual dynamite blasting as the great office-building boom engulfed Sixth Avenue; and Luigino's in the end went, too.) But this pizzeria was closed. Rye Beach has a short strip of stores, houses on both sides of 1A, and an unfancy beach of gray sand. On the section of it called Jenness Beach, three girls—undeterred by state law—were keeping their eyes on a half-gallon bottle of red Paisano cooling in the foamy edge of the sea.

One doesn't get a great sense of the past along much of this coast—perhaps because of the impact of the summery present, perhaps because the early settlers tended to make their first settlements farther inland (Rye preceded Rye Beach; Hampton, Hampton Beach, etc.)—but Straw's Point, which I was approaching, has not only a history but a prehistory. The section of 1A running up to it is called Cable Road, because in 1874 the first Atlantic telegraph cable came ashore at Straw's Point, from Ireland. The mansard-roofed, clapboard-sided cable station on Old Beach Road is now part of a motel, with bright-red doors and window trim. Before it was Straw's Point, it was Locke's Neck. One of the first settlers, John Locke, came on the canoes of an Indian raiding party here, cut holes in them, and caused the warriors to walk home. One day in 1694, they returned for revenge. They found Locke reaping grain and shot him with his own gun, which he'd left on a nearby rock. But before he died, Locke swung his sickle and cut off the nose of one of his enemies. A state historical marker on 1A near here draws attention to the fact that off the point are the remains of a sunken forest, remnants of the last Ice Age. Large gnarled stumps, with the original Atlantic cable weaving through them, are said to be visible at low tide. It was scarcely forty minutes after high water and I didn't see them. Deprived of pizza and blueberry muffins, and with hope of sustenance a mile away at Rye Harbor, I pushed on.

At 12:05 p.m., after more than eleven miles, I entered the first eating establishment I came to: the Rye Harbor Restaurant, which, for the purpose of taking in north-bound travelers, was strategically situated a quarter of a mile south of Rye Harbor itself. Instead of the harbor, a nutrient-looking marsh abuzz with birds and dragon-flies could be viewed through the screened restaurant windows. The décor within was seashore driftwood, with fishing nets and lobster-pot markers draped over cheap plywood paneling of the sort that looks like greasy brown linoleum, which was further enlivened with dreadful "original paintings" of schooners, draggers, yachts, and waves breaking on picturesque headlands. The paintings were for sale. However, I was the first lunch customer, and the young waitress—white dress, white shoes—was friendly. I had clam chowder, fried Maine shrimp, a bottle of Heineken's, and blueberry pie with vanilla ice cream—a dish which, in restaurants at least, is invariably better in the relish of anticipation than it turns out to be in the syrupy staleness of fact. (One of life's little lessons which I don't seem to learn.) When I paid the bill, the girl said, "Thank you very much, sir. Have a nice day."

The nice day I was having might have been even nicer if the road had not felt quite so hot through my sneakers. A little roadside marker informed me that 1A is called the Yankee Trail here, and I stepped along the edge of the trail, where tarmac thinned out into gravel and sand that was interwoven with lonely blades of coarse grass, hardy weeds, shreds of old beach towels and fiberglass insulation, fragments of brown beer bottles, and flattened Schlitz cans. The early Yankees dredged out the cove here for their fishing boats, and more recent improvers have enlarged it for yachts and lobster boats. A square bite out of the coast, partly closed by a stone breakwater, and with a few necessary sheds and buildings: that's Rye Harbor. I was glad to get onto the beach once more—first on the sands south of Concord Point, on Rye North Beach, and then, after another mile of roadwork, on the beach of Wallis Sands. Each of the New Hampshire beaches seems to lie between similar rocky points and to have a crescent of summer cottages, changing rooms, lifeguard chairs, flags flying above a club or pavilion, and kites flying. But Wallis Sands had a somewhat more intimate family scale than the others. Small children were kneeling, digging deep holes toward China, or sitting with their knees up, patting the sand into the shapes of forts or fishes—one was making a complacent-looking shark. It's nice to see people lying on beaches, face and stomach up, accepting the blessings of the sun, or face down, dozing in the warmth of it. One small child lay bottom up alongside his mother, an arm stretched across her back so that his fingers lay flat in total contact with her skin. A young couple—he in swimsuit, she in halter-neck top and denim shorts—lay face to face, kissing lightly, as if not to get each other sticky or sandy. In the sand nearby, someone had carefully written, in large capitals, DRACULA LIVES FOREVER.

At Wallis Sands, I perched myself on a flat stone, took off my sneakers, and stuck my feet in the sea. Lovely feeling! From my chart, it appeared that the rest of the coastline was rocky; it was going to be edge-of-the-road work for me from here on. Off Portsmouth, the tanker was still there, closer now, but looking as if she were lower in the water. One remarkable thing about this coastline is the lack of oil or tar on it, compared with any British or European beach, where small black globules of the sticky stuff are liable to get on your clothes or skin, and take a lot of getting off. How long this state of Eden will last, who knows? The *Union Leader* that day had a story about five of the six New England governors (free-living New Hampshire for some reason didn't participate) asking for a delay before they responded to a government request for their nominations of areas off their coast that should be preserved from oil drilling. (The governors were waiting for results of studies on fish population and ocean-bottom conditions.) Here the Isles of Shoals were at their closest. Sunlit yellow sand and green hillsides were visible on Appledore, the largest of the islands. Several white-sailed yachts leaned from the afternoon breeze. Small waves splashed over my feet against the rocks.

Undoubtedly, it is the sight and sound of natural movement, the perceptible evidence of time passing, that makes anyone sitting by the sea brood, or, as the poets used to put it, "muse." A century ago, John Greenleaf Whittier was the prime example of this activity in these parts, and wrote a number of now scarcely readable poems (mélanges of earnest newspaper editorials and women's magazine stories in strict meter) with such titles as "Hampton Beach" and "Amy Wentworth." Matthew Arnold's "Dover Beach" is the inimitable star of the genre, rendering, as it does so precisely, the way in which "the tremulous cadence" of the sea, with its "melancholy, long, withdrawing roar," who picked it in 1623 as a "fitt place to build their houses for habitacons" because "it was high, it had good harbor and a fine spring, and the great salt marsh to the west made it easily defensible against savages." The road wound beside the wooded crest of Odiorne's, on the right, and the wide salt marshes, pale green with the afternoon sun on them, stretching away to the left. Along here, I had to make a decision I had been putting off; this involved answering the question: Where does the New Hampshire coast actually stop? In many ways, Odiorne's Point has a good claim to be its termination—and I could have walked out along a little road that ran through a state park to the point, the end of the continuous mainland coast. But my chart showed that New Castle Island, to the north, had a small peninsula sticking out a smidgen to the east of the most easterly point of Odiorne's. It seemed that if I had stood out on the tip of Odiorne's and leaned well forward, I—or my nose—would have been as far east as that New Castle peninsula. There was also the fact that the geological-survey map, showing state borders, made it clear that New Castle Island lay cheek by jowl with the Maine border, running down the Piscataqua River; whereas Odiorne's Point was three-quarters of a mile from this frontier as it ran out to the Isles of Shoals. And there was an even more serious aspect of the situation. Although I sat pondering the problem some two miles as the crow flies from the Ultima Thule of New Castle, the route I would have to take to get there, around various bays and inlets and across bridges, looked to be at least five miles. I and my leg muscles had a little tussle with my conscience then. No one would dispute that—having reached Odiorne's—I had conquered the New Hampshire coastline, would he? *Would* he?

It was the inner glow of glory, therefore (and the fear that I might be denying myself a just helping of it), that kept my feet going. I trudged past Odiorne's Point and westward past Frost Point, and over the bridge that spans an inlet from Little Harbor, which takes a considerable chunk out of the marshes and had to be rounded. I was no longer quite so observant of roadside detail. I failed to proceed farther than I had to off my route in order to see the house, on Little Harbor Road, the WPA guide informed me had been the summer residence of Francis Parkman, the great nineteenth-century historian, and before that had been the home of Benning Wentworth. Benning was one of three Wentworths who were Royal Governors of New Hampshire—in his case, from 1741 to 1767. He held court here (the guide informs us) "in high-spirited style, keeping up the aristocratic tradition of bees-wing port and high play at cards . . . At the close of a banquet celebrating his sixtieth birthday and attended by the cream of New England's aristocracy, he called in Martha Hilton, his housekeeper, and bade the Reverend Arthur Brown, rector of St. John's Church in Portsmouth, read the [marriage] ceremony then and there, which the astonished prelate did." Thomas Bailey Aldrich, the Portsmouth writer (*An Old Town by the Sea*, 1893), called the house "an architectural freak" and "a cluster of whimsical extensions." He went on, "It originally contained fifty-two rooms . . . The chambers were connected in the oddest manner, by unexpected steps leading up or down, and capricious little passages that seem to have been the unhappy afterthoughts of the architect. But it is a mansion on a grand scale, and with a grand air. The cellar was arranged for the stabling of a troop of thirty horse in times of danger."

Route 1A went on into Portsmouth, and a mile or so

before reaching that city, I turned off on 1B. This ran past an occasional elderly private house and Mike's Marina, with a motley collection of old boats no longer in their element. Other boats were moored in the creek beside the bridge on which I crossed to New Castle Island. And there, overlooking the harbor and a golf course, was a sight! Why it isn't listed among the seven wonders of the world—or, at least, of New England—I don't know. But I nominate the Hotel Wentworth. It must be one of the largest clapboard buildings extant. Built in the 1870s, four stories high, with towers at both ends and a Swiss-chalet roof, it stretches—like the Empire State Building lying on its side—about a quarter of a mile along the road, which has the feeling here of being part of the golf club, with golfers and caddies strolling along it. At the Wentworth in 1905 stayed the delegates of the peace conference that brought to an end the Russo–Japanese War. Walking by it, I felt a bit dizzy, perhaps from the scale of the building, the light on the white clapboards, the weird vocabulary of golf that came to me in snatches, and the fact that I was moving on fast-running-down reserves of energy. I felt overwhelmed by surreal images of sunlit clarity, as in a Magritte—one such vision being of the battleship *Potemkin* planked in clapboards and manned by Lilliputian golfers.

Fortunately, it was only another mile or so, through a wooded area of prosperous, tucked-away exurban homes, into New Castle. Once a busy fishing community and military post, it is now a rather somnolent, fixed-up place, with narrow, winding streets that feel like mere paths widened by use. Old saltbox houses sat on grassy banks. But there wasn't much to suggest that New Castle was formerly the seat of the Royal Governor and his court, a town with crowded docks, taverns, and prisons; or that in 1682 the place was enlivened by the antics of a stone-throwing devil, who (according to Richard Chamberlain, Secretary of the Province at the time) "threw about, by an Invisible hand"—and particularly at one George Walton and his family—"Stones, Bricks, and Brick-bats of all sizes, with several other things, as Hammers, Mauls, Iron-Crows, Spits, and other domestick Utensils." The only thing flying in New Castle as I hobbled through it was Old Glory, the only noise the ping of halyards against the aluminum flagpole at the Coast Guard station. Here, overlooking the pretty, half-mile-wide Piscataqua toward Kittery, Maine, with Portsmouth and the navy shipyard just out of sight behind numerous small islands, a mile upstream, and to the southeast the mouth of the river and the Isles of Shoals, stood the military buildings and fortifications of several epochs. There were concrete bunkers of a battery put up during the Spanish–American War; a modern, glass-windowed control tower standing near a helicopter pad; the stone walls, with empty window embrasures, of an uncompleted Civil War fort; and, from before the Revolutionary War, the brick-and-masonry walls and bastions of Fort Constitution. I entered the last through a gateway with a wooden portcullis, recently replaced by the New Hampshire Daughters of the American Revolution—an anniversary present celebrating events in December of 1774, when, stirred by an early Paul Revere ride to Portsmouth to say that the British weren't going to allow any more military stores to be shipped to the colonies, four hundred local "patriots" overpowered the five-man British garrison of the fort, then called William and Mary, and carried off, among other things, a hundred barrels of gunpowder, put to use later on at Bunker Hill. This enterprise, says a handy sign, was one of the first overt acts of the American Revolution.

The fort is nicely bare, with crabgrass growing in the open space between the low battlements. I walked through the fort and the adjoining Civil War fortifications and out along a little gray-and-white painted wooden catwalk to a small lighthouse. This was it—the end of the coast. Five o'clock. Gulls and lobster boats made their rackety, preoccupied pronouncements; the big tanker, closer and even lower in the water, either sinking without making a big thing of it or taking on fuel through an unseen pipeline; vivid blues and greens and bright white-gray of sun on rocks. I took a long, sweeping look to stick it all firmly in my mind, and then started back through New Castle, putting to use the good old thumb.

IRISH MILES

THE SHANNON and the Bann are longer. The Lagan and the Liffey are better known, and debouch in Belfast and Dublin, respectively. The Moyle and the Lee, the southern Blackwater and the Barrow have their admirers. But the Boyne, which is neither large nor swift-flowing, is preeminent among what Louis MacNeice called the fermenting rivers of Ireland, in that it runs not merely through the mild countryside of County Meath but through the visible evidence of several millennia of Irish history. The river's name derives from Boann, one of the chief goddesses of pre-Christian Ireland. Like the Jordan, the Boyne is a holy river, figuring as such in Irish mythology and Ulster sectarian polemics. It rises thirty miles or so west of Dublin, and for seventy miles takes a semicircular course—roughly north, northeast, then east—to reach the Irish Sea at Drogheda, a town halfway between Dublin and the Northern Ireland border. It flows out of the green midlands of Ireland through some of the richest farmland in the country, and consequently from the first it has attracted invaders, settlers, and colonists, who have left along its banks reminders of their existence. The river springs from a source, near the tiny village of Carbury, known as Trinity Well, whose waters, like those of most of the three thousand holy wells of Ireland, are said to have special powers. Soon enlarged by small tributaries and the overflow from the great Bog of Allen, the Boyne heads north under the aqueduct of the disused Royal Canal and the Galway–Dublin railway. The first town it reaches in an as yet uneventful passage is Trim.

It was at Trim that Seamus Heaney and I began a late-June walk along the Boyne. Heaney is an Irish poet and teacher; he had just assessed the year's work of his students at a teacher-training college in Dublin, and his wife, Marie, examining a winter's growth in the poet's girth, believed that a few days' walking would do him good. He had a lecture on Wordsworth and Yeats to deliver at University College, Dublin, at eleven-thirty on a Wednesday morning, and then could get away. John O'Doherty, a teaching colleague of Heaney's, offered to drive us to Trim (the two daily buses from Dublin left inconveniently in the early morning and evening), and we accepted, though this meant abbreviating the post-lecture, preprandial gin and tonics at UCD—a session that might well have continued at Hartigan's or O'Dwyer's or wherever the Dublin midday is stretched into the afternoon by words and booze, and at which our expedition, for the moment barely hinted at as "Oh, just a stroll in the Boyne Valley," might have come to be not only delayed but regarded as something significant and symbolic and perhaps not altogether welcome in those competitive purlieus: an Irish poet originally out of the North and an English prose writer fraternally reconnoitering the sacred waters of the Boyne!

John O'Doherty's Honda got us swiftly away from these hazards. We ate sandwiches en route and, setting foot in Trim at two-thirty, made at once for a shoeshop so that Heaney could buy some boots. I was wearing a pair of leather L. L. Bean walking boots, well broken in. I recommended (remembering their breaking in) that Heaney buy footwear that could be worn comfortably at once, and, with this rather than looks or durability in mind, he purchased a pair of rather rakish off-white boots with "Dr. Marten's" stamped prominently on their sides, as if they were ships needing names. They would look all right, he thought, after he had stepped in a few cowpats. At the sweetshop next door, we bought ice creams, to give us impetus, and then we bade farewell to O'Doherty (who was carrying Heaney's old shoes back to Dublin) and set off through Trim. It was trying to rain. I wondered whether Sterne's Corporal Trim, in *Tristram Shandy*, hailed from hereabouts or whether it was simply as an authority on Ireland that Sterne invoked him when he had him say, "The whole country was like a puddle." Heaney said— bearing in mind the therapeutic reasons for this exercise—that he had to get out of Trim before he could get into it.

Trim *is* trim. A small market town, which won the Irish Tourist Board's Tidy Town competition in 1972 and again in 1974, the place, with little shops whose names are often lettered in a snaky Gaelic display script, has the air of a country town of fifty years ago. Tractors trundled up the main street, and people looked at us with interest, knowing we were strangers. Many of the buildings were of gray stone under gray slate roofs that glistened in the light drizzle. It was wet enough to make me put up my umbrella. I had on my back a green nylon knapsack, while Heaney carried his gear in a single-strap canvas bookbag, at first over one shoulder and then, when this proved uncomfortable, with the strap bandolier-style across his chest, holding the bag in midback. Seeing a Tourist Information Office, we went in and asked the colleen in charge for details of hotels and inns in Navan—our objective by nightfall—and for directions on how to find Trim Castle and the riverbank, along which we hoped to walk to Navan. The Navan hostelries were named and noted. The castle and the river were, sure enough, just around the corner. We purchased a little guide to the town. But the riverbank walk—that was obviously a question the girl hadn't been asked before. It was, she thought, "difficult." Would we let her know how we made out?

Trim's glories are its ruins. It has two ruined abbeys, a ruined friary, and ruined town walls and gates. Large sections of the walls were demolished by the Big Wind, a huge storm that did damage all over Ireland in the early nineteenth century. The present cathedral is a reduced but still splendid edifice called St. Patrick's. There is also, outside the walls, a turn-of-this-century St. Patrick's Church whose marble altars were made by Pearse Brothers, of Dublin—one being the father of Patrick Pearse, leader of the Easter Rising of 1916. In the grounds of this church in August 1978, a young British Army lieutenant was shot and seriously wounded while posing for wedding photos with his bride, a local girl who had been working as a nurse in London. He had done several tours of duty in the North. The Provisional IRA, which claimed responsibility for the deed, are thought to have a number of "volunteers" living in the neighborhood of Trim, carrying on the tradition of fanatic and militant opposition to both "invaders" and recognized government which in former times caused those in power to build structures like Trim Castle.

The castle is Trim's principal ruin, the largest medieval fortification in Ireland—and several thousand castles or tower houses were built in the country between 1150 and 1600. It stands in a field sloping down to the Boyne, which runs shallowly through the middle of town. Faced by another ruin in another field on the far bank, the castle has been much worked upon by time, gravity, various military ventures, and the Big Wind, which disassembled a large section of the curtain wall. (Cromwell's men, besieging the castle in the mid-seventeenth century, brought down a smaller section.) A greensward skirts the remains of the great stone keep, built in two stages by Walter de Lacy and the Crusader Geoffrey de Geneville between 1220 and 1225. On the grass lay a dozen cows, their recumbent attitude furnishing indubitable proof, Heaney and I agreed, that my umbrella was a good thing to have along. In an excavated area southwest of the keep are believed to be foundations of the first keep, built by Hugh de Lacy in 1174, an act recorded in an account of the Anglo-Norman invasion of Ireland called "The Song of Dermot and the Earl":

> *Then Hugh de Lacy*
> *Fortified a house at Trim*
> *And threw a fosse around it*
> *And enclosed it with a herisson.*
> *Within the house he placed then*
> *Brave knights of great worth.*

The Anglo-Normans were brought to Ireland in a manner similar to that in which the Angles and the Saxons were originally brought to Britain. They were invited first of all as allies by Dermot MacMurrough, of

Leinster, who was fighting Rory O'Connor, of Connaught, for the high kingship. The Anglo-Normans (who were French-speaking) soon took over much of the country, under the overlordship of King Henry II of England, and were soon feuding among themselves, like the Irish kings, and in sore need of their castles.

Famous visitors to Trim Castle at different stages of its development and devastation have included King John, who came with a suitable army to visit his Irish barons; King Richard II, who was here, fighting his Irish wars, when his rival Henry Bolingbroke staged a coup d'état in England; and Henry V, who stayed here as a child of eight. Across the river, in what was by turns an old abbey, a house, a private school, and then a house again, lived, in 1718, Esther Johnson—Swift's friend Stella. Arthur Wellesley, later Duke of Wellington, went as a child to the school; he was afterward the Member of Parliament for Trim, and as Prime Minister steered through the 1829 Act of Catholic Emancipation giving Catholics the right to sit in Parliament—which the Irish, since the Act of Union of 1800, had shared with the English at Westminster.

Just after three, Heaney and I sallied forth from the castle precincts, heading east. The rain was holding off. We took one backward look at the castle against the gray sky and strode forward in the direction of the riverbank, where a solitary figure stood—a young man, as we saw at closer range, with a surveyor's tripod. We asked him about walking conditions between here and Navan. He looked doubtful. There were lots of ditches and streams coming in to join the river, he thought. It might be better beyond Navan, where he had heard there was a towpath to Slane next to the abandoned riverside canal. As for his tripod, which we inquired about, he was surveying for a new road bridge, which would bypass Trim. The Board of Works (he said) had recently been dredging the Boyne along here, getting much silt out of the riverbed and exposing shelves of stone—an activity that stirred up the water and added oxygen to it, to the benefit of fish (and fishermen).

The path was blocked by a fence, a garden, and a large "Private" sign, so we made a detour across a field and walked up the road, which ran parallel to the river. Just before a bridge at a place identified on the map as Newtown Trim, we paused at a gate in a stone wall. "The Echo Gate," the Trim guidebook calls it. From it there was a view across a field and the Boyne to a ruined monastery on the far bank. Newtown Trim was a medieval suburb, it seems, and is now largely ruins. Heaney leaned over the gate and called out across to the monastery, "Go home!" The echo came: *"Go home!"* "Good gate!" called Heaney. A second or so later came the hollow reply: *"Good gate!"* "Cistercians—Trappists— silence!" shouted Heaney, getting into the swing of it. ". . . *silence,*" replied the echo.

I judged that to be a good exit line, and walked on toward the bridge, Heaney following, reluctant to leave this poet's plaything. At the bridge, a fine piece of medieval masonry, a few people were fishing while their children played on an adjacent ruin, the Crutched or Crossed Friary, so named after the friars or knights of St. John of Jerusalem, who formed a medical corps for crusading armies, wore a red cross on their uniforms, and after the Crusades set up a hospital here. For half a mile beyond this pile of stones, Heaney and I succeeded in following the riverbank. In the river, there were occasional natural weirs—stone ledges, outcrops of rock, and little islands, among which the silver-green

Boyne waters tumbled. We passed a woman fishing from the bank. She had long red-gold hair, and didn't turn her head as we walked behind her swishing through the grass, tall nettles, and flopping poppies. I was thinking that this was a fine symbol of woman's emancipation—spending the afternoon fishing—and looked at Heaney. His eyes were narrow slits. I wondered what he was thinking about. Boann, perhaps. She ought to be here.

For a while, the sun almost came out. Yellow-lit gray clouds scudded before the southwest wind, which was at our backs. We made our way along the edge of a meadow, which a farmer was mowing with a tractor, and clambered down into a gully where a small brook rushed in to join the Boyne. The Knightsbrook River, said my Irish Ordnance Survey map of the County of Meath. The Knightsbrook runs down through Laracor, two miles away, where Swift had a living and which he made his base from 1700 to 1713. The brook at first seemed impassable, but Heaney spotted a place with far-spaced stepping stones, meant perhaps for Brobding-nagian strides; we made it over. His Dr. Marten's were beginning to look less new.

Heaney was brought up on a farm in Derry; his father farmed and dealt in cattle. Heaney learned as a child how to mow and scythe, and how to milk cows. Now, at forty-one, in tweeds, and with a big-featured face, he looks more like a farmer than like a scholar-poet. ("Jaws puff round and solid as a turnip" are his own accurate words, in a poem called "Ancestral Photographs.") I am a generation further away from the land: my grandfather had a dairy and fields rented for his herd on the Isle of Wight, but insisted that my father, who wanted to be a farmer, enter a bank. When Heaney and I matched the names of plants and wild flowers we could see, he came out well ahead. There was mint and gorse, iris and forget-me-not, cow parsley and celandine; big oxeye daisies; meadowsweet and charlock; ragwort, herb Robert, yellow flag, and marsh valerian. Lovely words! Heaney told me some local names, such as "boor," which is what in Ulster they call the elder trees, thick along the riverbanks here, the white flowers on them looking, he thought, like full plates of meal. Vetch in Ireland is "robin-run-the-hedge." I thought the sound the river made was "running, running." And now we began to feel warm. It was still three miles to Bective, the next settlement. In Dublin, the pubs and bars are by law closed in midafternoon, the so-called holy hour. Heaney wondered if there was a holy hour in Bective.

We were now forced by wire and brambles and a deep, unbridged ditch to leave the river again, ascending a steep and overgrown bank and making our way along a thick hedge to the narrow road to Bective. And along here, after half a mile or so of roadwork, we came to a pump—a large iron pump, with a purposeful-looking curved handle, standing in a little concrete area at the roadside. We took turns at pumping and holding our mouths under the gushing spout—the water cool, with the definite stony taste of well water. Both Heaney and I were hung over. The previous evening had begun with a reading by the Irish poet John Montague at UCD and had continued with drinks at UCD, then at a bar, and finally at a bardic session at the Heaneys', fueled by wine and whiskey, that went on until 2:30 a.m. Montague and Senator Augustine Martin, a UCD professor, vied with each other for an hour in a duel of spontaneous chanting—making up a poetic dialogue of invocation, description, and abuse as they went along. This was followed by recitation, all present taking turns to speak their favorite poems of Yeats and Patrick Kavanagh, along with any other verses that came, fully or partly remembered, to their lips. The authors had to be guessed. I quoted now to Heaney, as the water splashed over his cheek, some lines from one of several poems of his that have pumps in them:

> *The helmeted pump in the yard*
> *heated its iron,*
> *water honeyed*
> *in the slung bucket*

We passed several small houses on this stretch. In the front garden of one cottage, a man was up a stepladder, cutting roses from a trellis. Everyone we had passed (save the woman on the riverbank) had given us a nod or hello, and this man was no exception. Heaney called out as we ambled by, "It's keeping up." The gardening man replied, "Oh, yes. You have it at your backs."

"We do, that," said Heaney.

"Are you going fishing?"

"No," said Heaney. "We're tormenting ourselves by walking."

"Oh, the fish are great in the river."

"Salmon?"

"No, the trout."

I had the feeling that we were upholding a tradition that the Irish—strangely, for such a tradition-bound people—were letting slip; that is, tramping, our possessions on our backs, a few things in our pockets, our heads in the air, and the country at our feet. Patrick Kavanagh, a country cobbler's son who became a farmer and then a poet, once went off tramping during a quiet spell on the farm. He set off in April with five pounds in his pocket and stayed two months on the road, getting back home in time to sow turnips, and cured of wander-lust.

As we came into Bective, we looked out over fields and slowly rising ground to the east and saw, three or four miles away, the Hill of Tara, dwelling place of the Dark Age kings of Ireland—a yellow-green ridge crested with a long clump of trees. But Bective itself at that moment interested us more: half a dozen houses at a road junction a few hundred yards from a bridge across the Boyne, and a general store, the left half selling groceries and the right half housing a bar, which was open. Here we shed our packs; here we sat down on barstools and drank a pint and a half apiece—I of Smithwicks bitter, and Heaney of Guinness stout. Three other customers were in the bar, all agriculturally clothed. One, to my left, was by himself, a taciturn fellow who grunted unin-formatively in reply to what I hoped was a friendly re-mark designed to open a conversation that might leave me wiser in local knowledge, particularly about which bank of the river to choose between here and Navan. On Heaney's right, the two other drinkers were talking quietly together, using occasional words like (Heaney reported) "redolence" and "sensibility." More farmer-poets? While we were there, Heaney used the phone to call a Navan hotel. Success! The Russell Arms would reserve some rooms for us. What was more, they served dinner until 11 p.m. Navan, by the river's bent-elbow route, was another seven miles. We ought to be there long before eleven.

It was, according to my watch, six o'clock. I looked at my watch because the clock over the bar, which had said a quarter past eleven when we came in, now said twenty *to* eleven. The second hand, moving counter-clockwise, confirmed the fact: time in the Bective bar, if not throughout the Boyne Valley, was moving backward. We grabbed our things and set off quickly, before we found ourselves even further back in the past than we had imagined ourselves to be. We traversed the bridge to the north bank (which looked like being better for the walk to Navan) and headed across a field stretching before the lovely ruins of a twelfth-century abbey: lichen- and ivy-covered tower, and loopholes, battlements, lancet arches, and the remains of a cloister. The Cistercian monks—obviously monks militant—possessed 245 acres hereabouts, together with a mill and a fish weir on the river and the right of their abbot to sit as a spiritual peer in Parliament. As we walked along the meadow edge, dragonflies darted out of the rushes along the river, ducks took off at our approach from the sliding river surface, and the blue-green reeds bent forward, dipping their heads constantly in the stream. After the open meadow, we came to a narrow bank on which thick woods impinged. The river wound into the distance of trees and fields and plantations, with the glimpse of a great house—Balsoon House, said the map—on the far bank. The map worried us by drawing our attention to the Clady River, a tributary due to spill into the Boyne any moment now. Anything called a river might take some crossing. However, when the Clady was reached, it proved no more of a hindrance than the Knightsbrook had been. A series of stones, not very evenly spaced, allowed us to hop over. Then the bank widened. There was gravel underfoot and, for a while, the sense of an old riverbank road. Swallows were swooping. I said, "If only they flew more slowly, so that one could see *how* they flew so fast"—a disjointed thought that Heaney fielded neatly, replying to me with Yeats's words, "I meditate upon a swallow's flight." Meditation was the only way of setting about it.

We brooded also upon derelict ancestral houses and their overgrown demesnes. We passed a long-disused stone slip in which a boat presumably had once been moored; hard by was a tumble-down boathouse. Midges in clouds betokened a fine day on the morrow (though it seemed a little soon after the recumbent cows to draw attention to this). Heaney spotted among the elder, alder, ash, and hickory growing along here a clump of bamboo, and cut himself a six-foot pole—something, he said, he'd always wanted as a boy, for a fishing rod. His country-man's acute eye also served me well. I was a pace or two in advance of him, and was just about to step into some thick brush overgrowing the path when he grabbed my shoulder and said urgently, "Look out there!" Prodding with his bamboo pole, Heaney pushed aside the brush and long grass to reveal a crevasse, a foot or so wide, into which I had been just about to walk—perhaps plunging (since no bottom was visible) into the Irish netherworld.

A little after seven-thirty, we reached a high stone bridge spanning the river, which here ran through a slight gorge. We decided to climb here and strike north to reach a road. Despite the initial suppleness of his Dr. Marten's, Heaney had a blister forming. Navan seemed distant and the evening well advanced, although, thanks to the northern summer twilight, it wouldn't be dark for two more hours. Irish miles had a separate legal existence until 1826 (when they were abolished); one Irish mile was approximately 1.27 British miles. They still feel longer. Perhaps this is so because one consults the Irish Ordnance Survey maps as if they were British maps, with the same scale, whereas the scale of the Irish is half an inch to a mile rather than one inch, as is most common in England. Consequently, what looks like an hour's walk is in fact two hours'. Moreover, when country walking, one finds no paths as straight as the routes that crows fly. One respects crops by walking the long way round the edge of fields. One follows meandering riverbanks and curving contour lines. And now getting up the embankment of the bridge took some zigzag climbing, effectively doubling the distance.

On the bridge, we walked out into the middle and sat for a few minutes looking upstream and down before bidding a temporary farewell to the Boyne. A grassed track ran across the bridge, which had once (we conjectured) carried a railway. Its course ran northward in a cutting that had become—as Irish land when left to its own devices often does—a sort of bog. Heaney, despite his blister, was in good spirits, possibly affected by the boggy ground underfoot. He has written a number of poems that have to do with bogs and with their preserving power, whether of food or implements or bodies that sink in them, and bogs have become for him a way of getting at and expressing in poetry the tenacious quality of Irish history—how so much that has happened in it keeps resurfacing, looking much as it did when it first went under. When the ground got too wet, we walked along one edge of the cutting. We noticed that the gateposts to a field were made of old railway ties. Rabbits scattered into the banks. After a mile or so with small farms on either side, we met a road. Under it, through a bridge, ran the former railway line, and there, on the far side of the brick arch, was the former railway station, spick-and-span, looking as if—save for the missing tracks—the 7:30 p.m. to Navan was about to come steaming in.

I went a bit astray at this point. I said we must obviously turn right on the road to get to Navan. Heaney said clearly we should go left. The station (in retrospect seen as having been done up as a house) disoriented me—gave me the feeling of being in another time and in an unexpected landscape. "Going astray" is not uncommon in Ireland. The phenomenon affects the natives, too. Some tell of getting into the middle of a well-known field and wandering around for an hour, maybe, unable to find the way out. Patrick Kavanagh and his mother went astray once while coming home in an ass cart from a visit to friends. All evening, in the rain, they drove around a skein of wet roads near Inniskeen, getting nowhere. "Everything seemed strange," Kavanagh wrote, in his book *The Green Fool*. "The folk we saw were not ordinary mortals." Finally, they decided to let the ass choose its own direction, and this worked. When they reached home, other traditional solutions to the predicament were proposed, such as turning one's coat inside out.

> "Paddy, ye were with the Wee Fellas," [one listener said].
> "Only for the ass we'd never escape," I said.
> "Indeed you would not," he supported, "sure the ass is a blessed animal."

After some dithering and discussion on the roadside, we went left, as Heaney had proposed, and soon met the Navan road. Possibly the railway station had been a figment. Perhaps I had been with the Wee Fellas. There was, however, nearly four miles still to go. The sky was darkening as the sun set, and gray clouds came in from the west. A mile along the lonely road, the rain began to fall. Umbrella up, coat collars up, we walked along, Heaney limping from his blister. We sang "It's a long, long way to Tipperary," and Kavanagh's "On Raglan Road," to the tune "The Dawning of the Day," which Heaney's wife, Marie, sings in a way to bring the moisture to your eyes. It wasn't long before the decision was taken, with one barely spoken accord, to try to hitch a ride into Navan.

Cars were infrequent on that road, but the goddess of the river was looking after journeyers that night: the second car stopped. Its driver was a friendly Australian, who dropped us right outside the Russell Arms Hotel in Navan. There the lady behind the reception desk—perhaps unused to guests who arrived with knapsacks and bamboo staffs, looking touched with the Meath greenery—asked to be paid in advance. But neither Heaney nor I reacted huffily to this suggestion. Hot baths and food and drink were in our minds. We paid up.

The Russell Arms: staircases going this way and that; the feeling of being in two or three large Victorian houses knocked together in a period of expansion, and now, that moment passed, in old age propping one another up. In the bathroom I used, there were no light bulbs in the fixtures and no plug in the bath. Fortunately, daylight of a feeble sort persisted. I used the small plug from the washbasin and added my facecloth to stem the ebb from the tub. In my bedroom, one out of three lights worked. However, on the ground floor all was well set up and jovial. The bar was full of early arrivals for a meeting of the local association of Tipperary Men—exiles, it appeared, from that fair county, all of a hundred miles from Navan. Heaney arrived, still hobbling, but otherwise restored by hot water. We drank apéritifs of Bushmills whiskey, from the North, and dined off sirloin, from the South. We toasted the Boyne with several carafes of red Spanish plonk. Meanwhile, the river was running a hundred yards away, unseen, past the backs of the houses of Navan, which resolutely look the other way.

We talked about the phrase "the Boyne." Where Heaney grew up and went to school in Northern Ireland, it was loaded with significance. For Northern Protestants, "the Boyne" connotes the battle in 1690 at which the troops of William III beat those of James II and thus kept all of Ireland firmly under British hegemony for the following two hundred and thirty years. In much of Ulster, to mention the Boyne is to reassert Protestant superiority. We swapped references that we recalled from ballads and folk songs—among others, "The Boyne Water" and "The Green Grassy Slopes of the Boyne," both of which celebrate Orange patriotism and William's victory. And the river's name occurs as symbol or metaphor in modern Irish poetry as often as blackbirds do in medieval Irish lyrics. The Boyne figures in the specifically Irish section of Louis MacNeice's long poem "Autumn Journal," where the poet (born in Belfast) evokes the yearly celebrations in Ulster on the anniversary of the Battle of the Boyne: "The voodoo of the Orange bands / Drawing an iron net through darkest Ulster." That section of the poem begins with a memorable ironic passage:

> *Nightmare leaves fatigue:*
> *We envy men of action*
> *Who sleep and wake, murder and intrigue*
> *Without being doubtful, without being haunted.*
> *And I envy the intransigence of my own*
> *Countrymen who shoot to kill and never*
> *See the victim's face become their own*
> *Or find his motive sabotage their motives.*

He wrote those lines in 1939–40, and it would be harder now, since the renewed Troubles and many deaths of the past ten years caused by terrorists, to use the word "envy" in that way—even though a sardonic tone comes through.

Tramping also leaves fatigue. Heaney and I retired before the bar called for last orders. I slept profoundly, and failed to hear the boisterous departure of the Tipperary Men, which Heaney next day reported as taking place sometime after two. He might have recalled a line of his own: "Drunk again, full as the Boyne."

Now Tara was our objective. We had bacon and eggs, the pleasure of no bill to pay, and lighter loads, for we left most of our gear at the Russell Arms reception desk. We walked up to the main square, a junction of four roads in the center of Navan, where we intended to catch the 9:20 Dublin bus as far as Tara, six miles south. Since we also intended to carry on walking after lunch along the next section of the Boyne, from Navan to Slane, we had decided that auxiliary transportation was permissible on this side jaunt. A number of people were already at the bus stop, but we had fifteen minutes in hand to try to find Heaney something easier on his back than his present bag; he was impressed by the lightweight, unstiffened nylon backpack I had bought for $4.95 in a Mystic, Connecticut, sporting goods store some years ago. Navan still had a saddler's shop, a hundred yards from the bus stop, whose dusty front window disclosed rugged brown suitcases, harnesses, and khaki knapsacks, none looking less than ten years old.

The venerable saddler took one of the knapsacks out of the window, shook the cobwebs off it, and strapped it on Heaney's back. "Ah, it's a wonderful fit, sir," he

said. The price for this piece of Old World craftsmanship,
an antique that had never been used, was, he added,
merely a fiver. "You'll take four pounds fifty," said
Heaney, astutely keeping any interrogative note out of
his voice, and staring intently at the knapsack's rusty
metal grommets. "Oh, it'll do you well. Just right for
tramping," said the saddler, as if he hadn't heard
Heaney's remark. But he gave Heaney fifty pence change
for the five-pound note.

The saddler's wife appeared in the back door to witness what might have been their first sale of the year—
or perhaps it was just the historic sight in Navan of two
tramping men.

At the bus stop, we joined the would-be passengers—
elderly men, middle-aged women, and a pair of girls
with most beautiful complexions. For entertainment
while waiting, we had the spectacle of three demolition
men at work on the Malocca Café across the square. It
was a strangely two-dimensional sight. The three workers, wearing woollen caps rather than hard hats, were
standing on the façade wall, all of nine inches thick,
above the second-story windows. There was no scaffold-
ing. The roof was already gone, and the men, carefully
wielding their pickaxes, were demolishing the wall half
a dozen bricks at a time beneath their own feet. We
waited for one of them to miss or lose his balance, but
none of them had done so by the time the bus came in.

The Dublin road first follows the Boyne south, upstream. Then, the river bending away westward toward
Bective, the road climbs the slopes of Tara. The driver
stopped the bus for us to get out at a junction with a side
lane, and we walked up this, still climbing. The lane was
narrow and heavy with hedges. The air was moist: not
quite raining, not even drizzling; simply wet. One could

see how things grew so well in Ireland, but one wondered how they ever ripened. From a nearby field came
the sweet smell of new-cut hay. Heaney said that his
friend David Hammond had told him the Vikings used
to coast along the land until they smelled hay, and then,
knowing that there must be habitations, would buckle
on their swords and come ashore. I said I thought the
east wind was the Vikings' wind, which filled their
square sails on the voyage westward from Scandinavia—
though no doubt they then coasted with the south-
westerlies, which carried the hay smells, first raiding in
Ireland and then settling to found such cities (trading
posts at first) as Dublin, Wexford, Waterford, Cork, and
Limerick.

Tara is a long hilltop; a windbreak of trees around an
old church and attached graveyard; and an extensive
meadow full of ridges, barrows, mounds, and earthworks.
"Tara" means a place with a wide view, and the hill,
rising three hundred feet or so above the general level
of the rich countryside, allows one to see over much of
the center of Ireland—yellow fields, green hedges, black
copses, and blue distant hills. Gray processions of rain
were marching along the Boyne Valley. Some parts of
the horizon were lost in mist or cloud, while others were
sunlit. Crows were strutting and cawing in an adjacent
field, while farther down the slope a man was driving
sheep across a pasture. The mist, reaching us, turned to
rain for a few minutes and then became mist again,
through which the sun tried to break. The grass was long
and wet, my boots not as waterproof as they had once
been. Heaney had the collar of his navy-blue raincoat
turned up, his tweed cap flat on his head, the empty
Navan knapsack on his back. We prowled around separately but occasionally converged on the same site: the

so-called Mound of the Hostages; the two long ridges believed by some to be walls of a great Dark Ages banqueting hall; and the mound encircled by twin ditches which is known as the rath—or fort with earthen walls—of the Forradh. On top of this are three pieces of stonework within an iron-railed enclosure. One is a five-foot-high upright pillar called the Lia Fáil—a stone on which the early kings of Ireland were allegedly crowned, but known to local Irish speakers in the nineteenth century as the phallus of Fergus. Another is a Celtic-style cross, with an inscription in Irish, put up to honor thirty-seven insurgents who died in 1798 during a skirmish with government forces in the Tara vicinity. The third is a mawkish statue of St. Patrick, bearded, with a bishop's miter on his head, right hand raised in unctuous blessing and his gaze firmly averted from the erect Lia Fáil. "The triple deities," said Heaney. "Though I suspect that in some ways the good saint here is a hybrid of the other two."

He sat down on a patch of dry gravel in the lee of St. Pat, with his back to the plinth on which the saint stood. St. Patrick was a Romano-Briton who is believed to have been carried off as a slave by Irish raiders at the age of sixteen, to have escaped after several years, to have studied in Gaul and been consecrated a bishop, and then to have returned as one of the first Christian missionaries to Ireland in the mid-fifth century. Like many other invaders, he made his way up the Boyne. At a hill over-looking Slane, Patrick (according to the earliest accounts, written roughly two hundred years after his mission) lit a great Paschal bonfire on Easter Eve. At Tara, King Laoghaire saw the fire ten miles to the north and took it as a challenge to his authority; it is said that he drove over to Slane in his chariot to give the intruder a dressing down, but he was himself let down by his followers, who received the saint's blessing and became believers. Patrick went on to appoint three hundred bishops, attached to ruling families, to carry out the peaceful conversion of Ireland; as far as one knows, there were no martyrs. Almost all the churches in these parts are named after him.

And what about these kings? The Gaels from Gaul who conquered Ireland in the first centuries after Christ became an ascendant class, providing perhaps several hundred ruling families. Ulster, behind its mountains and lakes, held out longest against the Gaels, the Ulstermen being led by Connor MacNessa, the Red Branch knights, and Cuchulain, the heroic Hound of Ulster. The Gaels provided perhaps a hundred and fifty "kings" in a total population of less than half a million. Professor James Beckett, the Irish historian, believes that by the fifth century there were seven provincial kings lording it over the petty kings, and that by this time, too, the king of Tara, one of the provinces, had put in his claim to be *árd rí*, or high king. But the high king's authority was nominal, despite his making a circuit of the island and exacting hostages from the smaller kings. One can see why so many children with Irish parents are told (as I was by my mother, a Molony) that they are descended from an Irish king; in my case, it was from Brian Boru, who fell at Clontarf, outside Dublin, in 1014, successfully defeating a Norse army. And the likelihood that these kings practiced polygamy increases one's chances of being of royal Gaelic descent.

Tara was abandoned as a royal site in the mid-sixth century. The collection of legends that provide the names for the mounds and monuments dates from written sources set down some four hundred years later; in fact, there are more names than monuments. Some archaeological work has been done, however, and excavation of the rath of the Synods (so called because of ecclesiastical meetings St. Patrick and other missionaries are thought to have held there) has shown that dwellers on the site had contact with the far-spread Roman world—a Roman seal, lock, and glass fragments have been found. Yet Ireland was never a part of that world (which is one reason the Dark Ages are so murky in Ireland); Irish ways were never tempered with Roman imperium or Roman law. And that there were kings on this spot seems supported by such finds as two gold torcs, now in the National Museum, Dublin. The kings apparently favored neolithic burial mounds for their habitations; at Tara, a Bronze Age passage grave (c. 2000 B.C.) has been found with pottery, bone pins, jet buttons, and a bronze awl of that period. Candy wrappers now decorate the ground at the grave's threshold.

When I returned to the rath of the Forradh after my reconnaissance, Heaney was still sheltering behind St. Patrick, jotting words in a notebook. A small military observation plane swooped low and circled twice, apparently observing *us*. "They must think we're an SAS detachment," said Heaney, who looked like a character from *Odd Man Out*, while I, in safari jacket and green jungle hat, was clearly dressed for counter-insurgency operations. Tara remains a commanding height. But we were, in any event, overwhelmed at this point by a busload of children, who came surging noisily over the site, dashing up the mounds and down into the ditches, the places of palisades and homes and graves. They ran to the enclosure where Heaney sat, and thronged round him. Suddenly among schoolchildren, he found himself answering their questions, telling them about the place, as if he were the genius loci. Indeed, the children seemed affected by the spot, as were we. Heaney had used in his lecture the previous morning the term "chthonic forces," which I later got him to define for me as the energies welling up from a place. The forces were strong here, at least in this weather of mist, showers, and watery sun: Cormac and Laoghaire, Fergus and Queen Maeve; the old peoples who lived and died here; kings on hills.

Before leaving, we looked in the little graveyard, where, among the Christian headstones, is a *sile* (or "sheila," as the word is pronounced): a gray rock face on which we could just discern in relief a female figure, knees spread wide as if making water on the ground— an image to avert evil or bring about fertility. In the Banqueting Hall Café, on the road where the school buses parked, we had a twenty-pence pot of tea, nicely timed, as the heavens opened and rain tumbled down. Then, with long slices of blue sky overhead, we went back down the rain-fragrant lane to the main road. It was eleven-thirty, and the next bus came by after one. So we walked along with our thumbs out and, after a while, got a lift into Navan from a heating-appliance salesman, who had what Heaney later called "a touch of the volubilities." In the car, he told us—learning that he was in the company of writing men—that he "used to read books."

After lunch at the Russell Arms, I donned my back-pack again. Heaney now had his fully loaded. The sun was mostly out still, and we went looking in Navan for the way to Slane along the river. We were misdirected at first by a local to the banks of the Blackwater, the river which joins the Boyne here, but we soon found some old stone steps beside a bridge spanning the Boyne, and these took us down to a path that ran between the

south bank of the river and a long-derelict canal alongside it, which in most places was full of reeds, rushes,
and nettles, and looked even less navigable than the river
it had been designed to supplant as an efficient waterway.
Over it stood small stone bridges with low arches, giving
just room for barges to get through. At intervals were
old locks, their gates and paddles collapsed and fallen in.
The canal was built between 1749 and 1800 to carry
coal, grain, and other mill products between Navan and
Drogheda, and most of its bridges and locks have inscribed on them the name of their designer, the engineer
Richard Evans.

Our path between river and canal was at first graveled,
then grassed, then overgrown. Heaney said, putting a
travel writer's tone of authority into his voice, "At
Navan, the character of the river changes." This stretch
of the Boyne gives the impression of having been worked
over by an eighteenth-century landscape architect. The
river is wider, with the Blackwater added to it. Great
stands of trees are growing in effective places, funnel-
ing the eye up green fields that roll away from the river.
There are appropriate ruins and occasional crags. We
met one man, hastening toward Navan, his breeches
and jerkin giving him the look of a gamekeeper, and
after him no one at all. The undergrowth, sometimes
growing over the path, became forbiddingly luxuriant.
Convolvulus grew larger, dock leaves were giant. We
saw a kingfisher as it zipped between the reeds—"like
blue voltage," said Heaney. The milestones that we
passed, giving the distance to Slane (ten miles by my
reckoning), appeared to be measuring the old Irish miles.
The wind was from the north, but the sun produced a
hint of summer heat. I kept a long stalk of grass in my
mouth; it was sweet at first, bitter if one chewed it.

Heaney moved with a sort of shuffle—tweed jacket, khaki knapsack, bamboo staff. I walked at a faster pace, and stopped now and then till he caught up, when he remarked about the advantages I had had of national service with a light-infantry regiment of the British Army. Heaney, a Catholic from Ulster, has had experiences of the British Army there, of being frisked and interrogated, that have left him not wholly sympathetic to Her Majesty's Forces, though he sees the difficulties of their peacekeeping role. In fact, many Irishmen, before and after Arthur Wellesley, have made a career in those forces. In 1914, the recruiting teams did good business in the South, and it wasn't just the men of Ulster who died at the Somme; the Irish Nationalist MPs William Redmond and Tom Kettle were among two hundred thousand Catholic and possibly Republican Irish who fought for the British in the First World War. My grandfather Frederick Molony served in the Royal Engineers. His sister Bessie was a nurse on the Western Front in the Queen Alexandra's Royal Nursing Corps. And his brother Tom died during the war in France from (his wife, Great-aunt Kitty, would always say) damp blankets.

Our histories are intertwined. The Boyne has relics of numerous ascendancies. Along here were more legacies of the French-speaking nobility who settled in the twelfth and thirteenth centuries in an area called the Pale. Beyond the Pale were what Shakespeare's Richard II called the "rough rug-headed kerns," and even within it each lord built his house as a castle, fortified against the peasantry, rival lords, and the king. In this landscape, the ruined castles had the air of follies, designed or deliberately ruined to fulfill an idea of the picturesque. Dunmoe Castle, which we passed near Milestone 4, was such a place. Said to have been built by a de Lacy, it last withstood siege during the Roundheads-vs-Cavaliers civil war, was restored during the reign of James II, and burned more or less down in 1799. When Sir William Wilde, Oscar's father and a well-known Dublin eye surgeon and antiquary, came past here in the 1840s, on a journey of research for a book about the Boyne and the Blackwater, he was told by the peasantry that an underground passage led from the castle under the Boyne to the opposite bank. As we went by, the wind passing over the two castellated towers or through the high empty windows sounded as if someone were blowing over the top of a huge bottle. Between us and the castle, on the north bank, the river fell over a small cascade; the water slithered sideways as it went down. A little farther on, we passed, on our bank, a ruined church, high on a slope over the river, and then a more contemporary structure—a small corrugated-steel shed, possibly for fishermen, on the river's edge. It was nicely provided with no lock on the door and straight-backed chairs, on which we sat outside for a while and watched the Boyne glide, like a smooth moving carpet, over a weir. For such a calm and purposeful operation, the resulting falling-water noise was surprisingly loud.

The temperature went up and down five degrees as the sun went in and out; the path moved away from the river through fields: cowpats, a pheasant, a herd of Jersey cattle, half a dozen handsome horses. The next landmark, halfway to Slane, was Stackallan Bridge, which like most Boyne river crossings has nearby points of interest: here a wayside monumental cross and a holy well dedicated to St. Patrick. We rashly assumed from the map that the path now shifted, as the canal did, to the north bank; apparently, the towing horses would be loaded aboard the barges, and then barges, cargo, and horses would be poled across the river and into the lock on the other bank. We therefore crossed the bridge. Heaney, parched, went to get a drink of water at a nearby house, and brought back the information that it should be possible to reach Slane on this bank, but no promise of how easy it would be.

In fact, the path was soon densely overgrown. An unknown plant, a cross between a mammoth dock and giant rhubarb, had settled here in thick colonies, rising to five or six feet and spreading out huge, salad-bowl leaves. It had to be beaten aside. Over these plants we glimpsed a fine ruined mill on the south bank, next to a splendid horseshoe-shaped weir. Then we were within a few feet of the river itself but couldn't see it. A short clearing gave us hope, but we were at once in jungle again. My boots were soaking from the wet grass. Heaney and I took turns in the van, bashing away at the plant life— not just the Triffid-like things but briars, thorns, and saplings. I broke off one of the last to use as a device for parting the way ahead. We needed machetes. We needed more energy than we had. We were being turned green by the Irish jungle. No one had been this way for years, or several seasons.* We were wet from below and getting wet from above as rain fell and haphazardly penetrated the forest. It was too thick for my umbrella to be of use

---

* Or possibly since Sir William Wilde journeyed here in the 1840s, and in the fashion of the time eulogized the landscape, particularly the bank we were on, "where groves of noble beech trees and aged chestnuts fringe the heights, and an underwood of laurels, thorns and sweet-briars mantle upon the undulating surface of the shores beneath . . . Here the river forms a number of sudden curves, each winding presenting us with a new picture more beautiful than its predecessor. The banks spring high and abrupt from the water's edge, so that in some places the massive trees, rising in piles of the most gorgeous foliage, appear toppling over us from their summits, and darken the deep smooth pools they overhang."

unless we stood still. When we halted for this purpose for a few minutes, Heaney sat down to rest on an ivy-covered log, which—rotten—crumbled under him, leaving him on the ground; he stayed there.

"You look like Sweeney," I said. He took it as a compliment. Sweeney was an Irish petty king or warlord, the subject of an early-medieval Irish poem called *The Frenzy of Sweeney*, which Heaney is slowly making a version of, called *Sweeney Astray*. Sweeney's problems begin when he is cursed by a local saint and finds himself flying round Ireland, nesting in hedges, treetops, and ditches—in the process speaking, as what Heaney has called "a tongue of the land," some of the most beautiful lines that have been written in description of the Irish landscape. We needed some of the bewitched king's powers now to get up into the tops of the trees and zoom out of this. And, indeed, when the last remaining suggestions of a path came to an end and the vegetation ahead looked impenetrable, we decided that it was time to be flexible about our intention of walking along the Boyne to Slane. We fought our way up into the woods, dragged ourselves up the steep ascent, and found—blessed relief!—open fields. Heaney was suffering not only from the previous day's blister but from an old thigh injury, acquired on the school football field, and, unable to get over barbed-wire fences, had to work his way under them. But we made it into the fields and along their southern edge, and reached the parkland of old trees and rolling ground which is the demesne of Slane Castle, seat of the Earl of Mount Charles. "Demesne" is a fine word, from the French *domain*, and evocative of medieval estates. The present earl had worked briefly for Faber and Faber, Heaney's London publishers, and we hoped that this (and the fact that

Heaney had phoned from Navan to reserve dinner for us at the Slane Castle restaurant) would give us entrée if we encountered the earl's gamekeepers before we reached the Navan–Slane road. Luck was with us here, however, and also on the road, where a fine fellow stopped and gave us a lift the last mile into Slane.

Slane had 896 people in 1837 and 526 in 1861, after the famine years; at the last count, in 1971, the population was 483. It is a well-planned eighteenth-century village, with the unusual feature of four nearly identical Georgian houses built aslant the corners of the crossroads, where the Navan–Drogheda and Dublin–Derry roads intersect. It has two churches named after St. Patrick, and a hotel, the Conyngham Arms, which deserves more than the one Automobile Association star it displays. The rooms were clean and well furnished; all light bulbs and bath plugs were in place; the water was hot and the beer cellar-cool. Despite the fact that we looked, if anything, more shattered than the day before, Heaney and I were not asked to pay in advance for our rooms.

Slane was the home of the Irish poet Francis Ledwidge, who was killed in Flanders in 1917. Ledwidge was a gentle, nature-observant writer, in tone and spirit close to the English poet Edward Thomas, who also died in the First World War. In Slane, Ledwidge is commemorated by a plaque on the bridge across the Boyne, which bears four lines from his "Lament for Thomas MacDonagh," a poet and friend of his, who was executed after the Easter Rising of 1916:

> *He shall not hear the bittern cry*
> *In the wild sky, where he is lain,*

twenty or so other customers properly fed, joined us for the second bottle. He is a graduate of Harvard University, where he was known as Henry Slane; after working for Faber's, he was the Irish representative of Sotheby's. Then his father, Marquess Conyngham, who owns land in England and had potential problems with the Irish wealth tax, asked Henry—as everyone in Slane calls him —if he would like to take over the castle and its thousand acres and make a go of it. This Henry and Juliet were now doing. They employ thirty men and women in the castle and on the farm. Slane has its own dairy cattle, its own fishing rights, and its own game birds. The independence of its present owners is enhanced by its power plant—a private turbine producing electricity from the ceaseless Boyne. (This was installed by Henry's grandfather, who also made much money from a carpet works in Navan; the turbine has been stopped only once in forty years, for an overhaul in 1959.) Henry would have a seat in the British House of Lords when he succeeded his father, and he didn't disguise the fact that in running this sort of establishment for profit (which depends partly on the successful manipulation of the past, of associations, nostalgia, deference, and need for the unusual), a title—a "handle," as he called it—was very useful, though possibly the EEC's Common Agricultural Policy's effect on farm prices counted for more.

After dinner, Henry gave us a tour of the interior. Slane Castle is mostly a product of the late eighteenth century. Henry's ancestors, the Conynghams, were a Scottish family who came to Donegal in 1611. Sir Albert Conyngham fought for King William at the Boyne in 1690. On James II's side fought Christopher Fleming, the twenty-second Lord Baron of Slane, whose family had held the estates from 1175 until 1641, when they were confiscated and sold to the Conynghams. Bits of the old Fleming castle are believed to have been incorporated in the Gothic Revival house that James Wyatt, the architect, designed here, with mock battlements and corner towers, and set on a rocky bastion overlooking a bend of the Boyne. Francis Johnston oversaw its completion. Capability Brown did the stables. Henry has a telephone switchboard and a telex machine in his offices. Of the many elegant rooms, that which serves as both library and ballroom is perhaps the finest—a round room, with crimson walls and white plaster Gothic tracery on the domed ceiling. It was built especially for a visit by King George IV in 1821, and would undoubtedly have appealed to the patron of the Brighton Pavilion. However, the main appeal for George IV at Slane, it is said, was Lady Conyngham. One of the reasons that are traditionally given for the straightening of the Dublin–Slane road—it is one of the straightest roads in Ireland—was George's desire to get to Slane and Lady C. as fast as possible. In reality, though well acquainted with her by 1815, George is thought to have stayed at Slane Castle only twice—once before and once after he was crowned king. It was while he was dining at Slane that George, in fine spirits, suggested sending Lord Talbot, the Lord Lieutenant of Ireland, to look after England while he himself stayed where he was.

In the castle now are various prized mementos of these associations, and statues and pictures of the nobility England and Ireland shared, for better and worse. There is a portrait of the first Marquess Conyngham by Gilbert Stuart (George when he was Prince Regent not only got Lady C.'s husband this title but had him made Constable of Windsor Castle and Lord Steward of the Royal Household). And there is a full-length, life-size portrait of a handsome officer, the Marquess of Anglesey, who was also one of Henry's ancestors. It was at the Battle of Waterloo in 1815, as Henry reminded us, that the Duke of Wellington is supposed to have said to Anglesey, just after a cannonball whizzed by, "By Gad, Harry, you've lost your leg!" and Anglesey is said to have replied, "By Gad, sir, so I have."

Day three: a fine morning. Heaney had to be back in Dublin that afternoon for a meeting and was catching the Dublin bus at ten. He was, I suspected, pleased not to have to put his Dr. Marten's to the test for another day. After an excellent breakfast at the Conyngham Arms, we said goodbye. My boots had been put to dry on the kitchen range at the hotel, and though I went down to Slane Bridge for a glimpse of the distant castle standing on "its swelling bank of greensward" (as Wilde described it), and of the woods overhanging the river that had thwarted Heaney and myself the evening before, I decided to keep my boots dry for the moment by forgoing any excursions into the thick undergrowth between bridge and castle. I took on trust that somewhere in the wet, tangled shrubbery, under yews and beeches, was the ancient ruin known as the Hermitage of St. Erc. St. Erc, one of St. Patrick's right-hand men and the first Bishop of Slane, is said to have often stood for hours at a time in the chill Boyne waters in order to cool his concupiscent desires. From the bridge, alleged to have been a favorite haunt of Mick Collier, the last of the Irish highwaymen, there is also a spacious view downstream past Slane Mill toward the big bend of the river at Rosnaree. I returned to the village crossroads and marched forth on the Drogheda Road, spurning the temptations prompted by the Live and Let Live public house, and leaving over my left shoulder the hill on which St. Patrick lit his Paschal fire.

It was just gone eleven as I walked from Slane. It was fox-and-geese weather—the promise of the early morning already compromised by loose gray clouds scudding behind me, threatening showers. I was going to have to walk faster than Heaney and I had done to fit into this day all that I wanted, and I kept up a light-infantry pace for the first few miles, exercising the freedom of the road to whistle and sing, and swinging my umbrella at the trail, parallel with the ground. I turned right on the first minor road, which led toward the Boyne again and the great neolithic burial mounds of Knowth, Newgrange, and Dowth. A vole ran across the road; at a farm gate stood a pair of milk churns, awaiting collection. But, despite the rural signs, there were also short stretches of ribbon development, as there seem to be on many country roads in the east of Ireland—development, admittedly, that often appeared to be proceeding by well-spaced fits and starts. A few new houses here stood empty in plots alongside unfinished houses or old, completed cottages that had for some reason been long abandoned. To whom do these derelict or unoccupied dwellings belong? Will the new houses ever be lived in? Are there sons and daughters in Liverpool or Boston who will one day come to glaze the boarded-up windows and paint the pebble dash? To keep a cow or a goat in one of these small hedged fields?

Heaney had given me the name of the archaeologist, Professor George Eogan, who is in charge of the excavations at Knowth. At the top of a rise, opposite a farmhouse, I came to a high wire fence, through which I could see the huge tumulus, with parts of the covering turf peeled back, and black Polythene protecting some of the excavated ground. I let myself in through a gate and, walking past a pile of spades and picks next to a fork-lift truck, found the prefabricated hut which was site headquarters. There I introduced myself to Dr. Eogan, a sharp-eyed but genial man in his fifties, who has been working on Knowth since 1962, digging during the summers with his students from University College, Dublin, and, during term time, sorting out the results back in the city. A postgraduate student, Aideen Ireland, gave me a tour of the excavations, starting at one side of the central mound, where we walked cautiously on thin ridges of earth left between four-meter-square excavation pits, in which the diggers were working with tiny trowels and toothbrushes, finding, if they were lucky, minute pieces of bone or bead.

The mound itself is a megalithic tomb containing two passage graves. Some three hundred such graves are known in Ireland, and those in the three mounds that form a great cemetery on the Boyne are preeminent. They date, my guide told me, from between 3000 and 2500 B.C. They are the works of a people about whom not much is known except on the basis of these tombs, but who could clearly gather their energies in a project that consumed much time and labor, and who honored their dead, installing the cremated ashes in shallow stone basins set in niches deep in the passage graves. The graves themselves were formed of huge stones. The mound covering those at Knowth extends over one and a half acres; it is some ninety meters in diameter and more than ten meters high. It is surrounded by a circle of large edgestones, decorated with incised motifs— circles, U shapes, diamond shapes, spirals, zigzags, and herringbones. The mound was carefully built in layers, thicker in the middle and sloping slightly downward toward the edges, presumably for better drainage.

We stood on top of the mound in the warm sun and cool breeze and looked out over the valley—to the flat-topped sister mound of Newgrange, a mile away; to the curving river and, beyond, to Tara; and to the Wicklow hills, visible beyond Dublin twenty-five miles south. It was obviously a good site—first time lucky, in a way, since these recently nomadic and hunting people were on the point of becoming farmers and herders, their animals becoming domestic. And settling down seemed to involve giving a permanent dwelling place first of all to their dead—levering tons of stone, slowly chipping away the magical designs with hammers of flint. The early Irish were diggers and navvies and artists. And, after the cremations and burials, the place itself was good for the living, then and thereafter, overlooking and controlling the fertile valley and the river, with its fish. In the Iron Age, people inhabited the mound itself, digging deep ditches round it and building stone walls on top. The Celtic invaders made this cemetery their Olympus, the home of their gods. The Vikings looted it and the Normans built a fort on it. In 1699, the Welsh antiquary Edward Lhuyd came to the Boyne cemetery, the first of a line of inquisitive scientists and excavators. In the eighteenth century, the locals dug here for handy road-building materials.

After thanking Miss Ireland and Dr. Eogan, I walked on down the lane to Newgrange. At a junction, I spurned the advice of the road sign—deciding, after a look at my map, that the sign proposed a route better for cars and longer for me—and, after a few minutes' doubt on the single-track road I'd chosen, had the pleasure of seeing

Newgrange appear again over the high hedges, several fields distant. All along here, the elder trees were in flower and blackbirds were singing, as they have in all likelihood since neolithic times to movers of stone, monks, farmers, warriors, and people walking down lanes.

I reached Newgrange at one o'clock. Newgrange has been excavated and restored, and sits dramatically in the middle of a wide field, with green grass all round, an immense wall of small white stones banked up on either side of the grave entrance, and half a dozen standing stones in front and one reclining, heavily incised stone as the grave threshold. Visitors are allowed to walk round and enter the passage grave. A party had just left, but one of the guides—girl students—kindly led me in. The huge stones forming the tunnel of the grave lean inward, the roof stones press down. We squeezed along the passage and into the chamber, where the space expands out into alcoves or niches and up into the corbeled dome. My guide, who was about twenty, leaned back against a stone and gave me a short speech: ". . . passage-grave makers, perhaps from Brittany . . . shellfish eaters . . . some four thousand years ago . . . burials . . . cremations . . . we don't know much about them . . ." How pretty she is, I thought. Was this the age-old conjunction of instincts—sex and death? She told me that at Newgrange on about December 21, the day of the winter solstice, the sun comes up over the eastern horizon and shoots a long shaft of light through a slit in the roof over the grave entrance and down the passage, lighting up the chamber for precisely seventeen minutes. This and the arrangement of standing stones outside suggested that the builders had astronomical knowledge and made calendar observations. She also pointed out the incisions in some stones; the triple-spiral motif, to be seen on several, was a subject of conjecture. I hazarded the idea that it might symbolize Knowth / Newgrange / Dowth. That, she said, was one of the conjectures.

Outside again: the breeze shaking the full-leafed trees along the lane, sun gleaming off the white stone embankment of the giant mound. I had neglected to bring any lunch. I lay on the grass and read some notes I had made from Dr. Michael Herity's treatise, *Irish Passage Graves*, in which, after much detailed scholarship, he lets loose:

The whole impression in the Boyne is of a township like medieval Florence, sure of its economy, confidently undertaking the erection of a great cathedral to ensure spiritual sustenance, at its head a ruler of wisdom, strength and leadership.

Dr. Herity believes that three hard-working communities lived in this area, compact enough to have a common purpose, each depending on the labors of some five hundred able workers to build its tombs, over roughly twenty years. He writes:

When death came, a great mausoleum was ready to house the dead, the spirit of the supernatural watching from its walls, its elevated site and the mass of its tumulus designed to awe the living. After the cremation ceremonies the ashes of the dead, borne in pottery vessels ornamented with the same symbols as those on the tomb walls and accompanied only by the ornamental miniatures they had worn in life, were laid to rest in the house they had planned and built.

There is a line in Lewis Mumford's *The City in History*: "The Egyptians loved life so much they even embraced death." I thought also of a poem Heaney has written, called "Funeral Rites," in which he imagines an immense funeral procession moving from Ulster to the Boyne, to—as he has said in a radio broadcast—"the megalithic burial chambers which were fabulous even in early Irish times. Then people thought of them as the burial places of heroes and semi-gods, but I think of them here as the solemn resting places for casualties, the innocent dead of the past few years."

I walked on, two miles to Dowth. This burial mound is unrestored, unexcavated since the nineteenth century, after which it became a grassed-over crater. No one was about. I stood on the mound and watched the wind move like a demonstration of energy through the long grass. As at Knowth and Newgrange, there was a fine view of the river half a mile away. Newgrange was in sight to the west. Just to the east, next to a ruined mansion, stood the shell of a church, and in the surrounding churchyard, just scythed, a man out of Brueghel was carrying hay on a pitchfork. As I walked back to the road, an elderly, well-groomed lady came by, walking her dog, looking as if she did this every day.

I had found a roadside pump just before Dowth. At it I had filled my grumbling stomach with well water, and this kept me going through the next few miles of warm sun and winding road toward Oldbridge. In the course of the next forty-five minutes, I was passed by two cars. I saw one man, a roadworker, pruning a hedge with a billhook beside a bridge where the little River Mattock runs beneath the road to join the Boyne.

"Keeping fine," I said.

"Yes, not so bad today," said he.

When the Boyne came in sight again, at the junction of the lane I was on and the Slane–Drogheda road, it was spread out and slow-moving. Fishermen were angling from the far bank. More ruined houses loomed through the trees. A midafternoon torpor overhung everything, but I kept going and at ten to three found myself at Oldbridge, where a narrow stone-and-iron bridge spans the river, and another era of Irish history is immanent. And there, too, on a wide grass verge, a piece of ground over which hundreds of troops charged toward the river one July day in 1690, sat a gypsy caravan. It was prairie-schooner-shaped but small. The panels on each side of the back door were painted red, yellow, gold, and green, like illuminations in the Book of Kells. A subsidiary dwelling had been set up on the grass nearby, a sort of nomadic hut made of canvas stretched over wooden hoops—indeed, it looked like an upside-down coracle. The canvas was partly rolled back to reveal bedding inside: mattress, several plump pillows, and an eider-down embroidered or patchworked with a magnificence to match the painting of the caravan. There was some-thing Oriental about these sparse but luxurious belong-ings. A goat tethered to a stake a few yards away was champing grass. Several horses, seemingly the steeds of the caravan's owner, were in an adjacent field. An iron pot hung from a tripod over a campfire. And in the grass a man lay on his back, holding aloft a baby. The baby was giggling; the man was uttering fond parental noises to make it laugh. I gave them a wave and a hail in greeting, and the man—after a solemn look, presumably to see that I wasn't an agent of council authority or the farmer who owned the field—nodded and smiled in return.

The tide reaches up the Boyne from the sea to this point. Walking onto the bridge, I concluded that the tide was out; this accounted for the present shallowness of the river. It would have been easy to ford, which was the reason William III chose it for one of his four river crossings on the morning of July 1, 1690, and the reason James II (who was with his staff on the slopes of Donore Hill, to the south) had many of his troops on the other bank, guarding the crossing. (July 1 was the date of the Battle of the Boyne in the old-style, Julian calendar. In the new-style, Gregorian calendar, adopted in the British Isles in 1752, the date is July 12.) In any event, when William realized that the ford at Oldbridge was well covered by the Jacobite forces, he smartly sent a large detachment from his ample army (35,000; James had 25,000) off westward to cross the river at Rosnaree, between Knowth and Newgrange. James thought this feint to his flank was the real thing, and diverted much of his Oldbridge force to meet them. William's deception plan succeeded. The diverting and diverted parties sat and faced each other across a bog all morning while William's main army came across the river at Oldbridge and met the rest of James's.

It was a European battle. William, Prince of Orange, Stadholder of the United Provinces, had been offered the British throne by those who wished to preserve the Protestant succession and constitutional monarchy. Catholic James, deposed in England, was making his penultimate stand in Ireland with French support. He had fighting for him Englishmen, Scotsmen, Irishmen, Dutchmen, and Frenchmen. William had Dutch, Germans, Danes, Scots, English, Huguenot French, and even some Catholic Irish. To tell each other apart, the Williamites wore green sprigs in their headgear, the Jacobites wore white cockades; but this didn't prevent allies from now and then fighting one another.

Across the bridge there is thick undergrowth on either side—a tough place for a skirmish. It was, one participant recalled, "an excessive hot day." When William's Blue Dutch Guards forded the river, they held their muskets and powder above their heads; as they came up the bank on this side, the fifes and drums were playing "Lilliburlero." I sat down by a desolate gatehouse at the first bend in the road and changed my socks—an old soldier's trick for the restoration of tired feet—rubbing my bare toes in the grass and airing them for five minutes before donning Mr. Bean's boots again. Road signs directed me toward the Jacobite camp, but after a mile or so of uphill plodding along tortuous lanes, I struck out across the fields to Donore Hill, whose summit was crowned by a clump of trees and a small walled cemetery. Among the obstacles were barbed-wire fences, deep ditches full of mud and nettles, thorn hedges, and fields full of cows and possibly one or two bulls; but eventually I was there, seated on the stone wall surrounding the graveyard. 3:50 p.m.

I had my jacket off for the first time on this walk. It was hot, but not excessive. I looked north, down the long slope of hillside on which the last stages of battle had taken place. To the right, three miles or so away, I could see the buildings of Drogheda and, beyond, for the first time, the sea; to the northeast, the mountains of Mourne. It was twenty miles from where I sat to the North–South border, along which there are still ambushes, booby traps, sudden murders, and the working out of old horrors. What is always impressive about battlefields is the fertility of the fields, the felicity of the countryside. But here, without much effort, I could imagine men in the ditches and hedgerows, pikemen holding off cavalry, the confusion of charges, retreats, and orders not getting through. Smoke—bayonets—musketballs—and a good deal of dying and injury less stoically received than Lord Anglesey's. The Jacobites lost nearly a thousand men and William some five hundred. (Even so, seven thousand of William's men had died from disease the previous winter.)

At Aughrim a year later, the Catholic army met its final defeat in Ireland, but this battle at the Boyne has always been considered the real defeat. James retreated that night to Dublin and took ship for France. And in the war of words that has been so much of Irish history, the Boyne is immortal. Most Irish schoolchildren were brought up to identify with one side or the other; the account of the Boyne battle in most Irish history books, until very recently, discloses the cultural, religious, and political bias of the author. Few Irish Catholic children are named William. The Protestant king spent only a fortnight in Ireland, but he became for Northern Protestants the symbol of the Irish-British Union. King Billy is the affectionate title they've given him, though at the time many of his supporters thought him cold and standoffish. He didn't speak English very well. And who knows if—as Ulster iconography insists—he actually rode a white horse on that day of battle? Many in the North, despite the ubiquitous slogan "Remember 1690" painted on walls and gables, have no clear idea of when the battle took place. Some believe it occurred in Biblical times. There is the famous story of the visitor to the North who is puzzled by all the references to King Billy and the Boyne, and asks an old Ulsterman what it's all about. He is told, "Away with ye, man, and read yer Bible!"

Celebrations of the anniversary of the Boyne battle were first held in the North in 1797, as liberal Presbyterianism began to be supplanted by the Orange Order and by a "No Surrender" attitude regarding the maintenance of a Protestant ascendancy. In 1914, that attitude was so entrenched that Protestant Ulster nearly revolted at the prospect of home rule for all of Ireland—a situation in which they feared they would be swamped by the Catholic majority. When it looked as if there might be a Unionist rising in March that year, British generals considered moving the Fifth Army Division from its camps in central Ireland to a line along the Boyne, facing north. But world war provided for the death of home rule—and in turn for the frustrations that helped produce the Easter Rising, in 1916. It was on July 1 (the old-style date of the Battle of the Boyne), 1916, that the Battle of the Somme began, and men of the Thirty-sixth Ulster Division went over the top wearing orange ribbons, shouting "No Surrender" and "Remember 1690" as they plunged into the German machine-gun fire.

That year, after the Somme debacle, there was no Orange parade in the North. But, except for that single omission, each July has seen an anniversary celebration of the Boyne victory. In Belfast, the parade takes two and a half hours to pass a particular spot, with drums throbbing and the fifes playing their shrill tunes. On this day of sashes and banners, the ministers preach and the politicians pronounce as to God's own, a chosen people. A notable example was the speech made on July 12, 1934, by Sir Basil Brooke, then Minister of Agriculture in Northern Ireland and later Prime Minister of Northern Ireland, which illustrates what Catholics in the North were up against for so many years. Sir Basil said, "Many in this audience employ Catholics, but I have not one about my place. Catholics are out to destroy Ulster . . . If we in Ulster allow Roman Catholics to work on our farms we are traitors to Ulster . . . I would appeal to loyalists, therefore, wherever possible, to employ good Protestant lads and lassies."

Possibly it is a sign of progress that, despite the last ten years of Troubles, that sort of statement, reflecting fairly widespread feeling at the time, could be made by probably only one Ulster MP today. And the Twelfth parade itself is no longer quite so fraught with religious or tribal hostility. Some young Protestants are forbidden to take part in it by parents who regard it as a manifestation of bigotry; some young Catholics begin to think of it as a sort of carnival. An increasing number of people are perhaps coming to share Conor Cruise O'Brien's feeling that the Irish have often in the past behaved "like sleepwalkers, locked in some eternal ritual reenactment, muttering senselessly as we collided with one another." (For that reason, O'Brien chose not to attend a ceremony commemorating the landing of arms from Erskine Childers's yacht *Asgard*—a ceremony, he thought, that merely underlined the ancient rivalries and passions.)

On the grassy slopes of the Boyne on a warm afternoon, topography is more impressive than history. This land is unlike so much of Ireland—a country broken up into areas of poor soil, barren mountains, and bog. The geographical fragmentation of the country has in the past been intensified by the use of the land and by a system of inheritance, in the words of the geographer E. Estyn Evans, that entailed "re-allocating land periodically among close kinsmen, and subdividing already scattered plots among co-heirs." Evans and others believe that such practices, over the centuries, have contributed to the violent feeling that lies just below the surface and has brought about so much internecine bloodshed in Ireland.

In the late afternoon, I abandoned my hilltop perch, my petty kingdom, and made my way across the fields to the lane again. It was two miles of country roadwork into Drogheda, a sizable market and manufacturing town built on both steep banks of the river. Drogheda is famous for its fortified walls, which the English Commonwealth troops of Oliver Cromwell stormed during the civil war in 1649, proceeding to slaughter the Drogheda garrison. Cromwell said, "Our men getting up to them were ordered by me to put them all to the sword." Cromwell saw himself not only as attacking royalists but as the instrument of divine vengeance against those Irish who had rebelled in Ulster in 1641. He wrote from Drogheda, "This is a righteous judgement of God upon these barbarous wretches, who have imbrued their hands in so much innocent blood." The effect of the death of the three thousand Drogheda men was to emblazon his own name in Irish memory as a butcher, and to associate his country with the act.

Drogheda is also noted for disputes about the pronunciation of its name, the English—including the Earl of Drogheda—going for "Drowda," which to me sounds Irish, and most of the locals calling it "Drockeda," which is direct enough. Until recently, communication from one side of town to the other was via a pair of narrow bridges, which had to carry not only local vehicles but much of the coastal road traffic between North and South. Four years ago, a new, wide road bridge was built, and was named by the Drogheda town council Peace Bridge. In December 1976, shortly after it opened, a rally was held on the bridge by the Northern Ireland Peace Movement, whose founders, Mrs. Betty Williams and Miss Mairead Corrigan, won the Nobel Peace Prize the following year. Ten thousand people turned up from North and South and in two columns—almost two armies—surged across the bridge from each side of the Boyne to meet in the middle, embrace, shake hands, or otherwise greet one another. The Peace Movement's leadership has recently been in disarray, and it has been criticized for failing to get support from the city ghetto-dwellers or for dealing in cosmetic solutions. But it seems to me that its dramatization of the possibilities of friendship has been important in a country where the last years have seen rather the reiteration of terror and animosity. Added to which, the Peace Movement has put some of its funds to very good use, by, for example, lending money to small companies that have been unable to qualify for loans from the government or banks. And it may be that one of the "solutions" for divided Ireland is the willingness to try all sorts of proposals, and to analyze and question all deeply ingrained attitudes and beliefs.

I walked across Peace Bridge and along the main shopping street of Drogheda. The fortifications, the cathedral, and the Boyne salmon curraghs (the last basketwork-and-skin boats in Ireland, I'd been told) would have to wait for another day. I was all tramped out. I inquired the whereabouts of the railway station, and, on learning that it was half a mile out of town,

asked about buses to Dublin; they, it appeared, were
not far down the hill, by the river. There, indeed, a bus
was loading up. I had just time to buy some chocolate
and apples from a nearby shop and to take a last look, as
the queue of passengers moved forward into the bus, over
the footpath railing at the Boyne.

PROMENADE

DES ANGLAIS

MONDAY: Sudden sunlight. The sharpness of it is unchanged. Only the means of getting here have altered. Today, the morning flight from London and a surly cab driver, suspicious of the airport-to-hotel transport voucher, provided by the travel agency, that I wave at him. He knows that it means *service compris*—in other words, no tip. Was it for this that he put imitation-leopard-skin covers on the seats of his Mercedes? He accelerates grumpily past palms, pedestrians, the seafront residences and hotels. In the back seat, I am separated from my companion by raincoats, magazines, a handbag, and other travel paraphernalia, but I feel that she is thinking of the last time we arrived here. Then it was the night train and cramped couchettes. There was little sleep to be had in the steel compartment, with its rattling bunks and the noises from other passengers, who included a young mother and her baby. Besides, on that previous trip I was bothered by the insistent memory that, the week before, the Nice–Paris express had come off the rails near Avignon, at 120 kilometers an hour, scalding to death a number of people in the carriage behind the engine. Lying on my berth,

I could imagine the headlines: RAIL CRASH—ENGLISH HONEYMOONERS AMONG VICTIMS. But travel on this route has always had its anxieties—the Channel packet, the lee rail, the entrance to Calais harbor (*vide* J. M. W. Turner's painting, which shows the frenzied overfalls, waves crashing on the breakwater, and the crazed look of the helmsman). For the next stage—well documented by Tobias Smollett, among others—the traveler hired a diligence for the long trip south and then had squabbles with the owners of horses and the *patrons* of *auberges*. Axletrees broke; wheels flew off; the postillion was struck by a sizzling bolt from the blue. And yet at last the coast, the sunlight, the azure sea. Romance! Twenty years ago, we sat drinking *café filtre* out of low white cups in the jouncing PLM restaurant car as it turned the corner at Marseilles and ran eastward past the capes and bays. Today, the Super Caravelle throttled back and came down through thin cloud, jolting as the undercarriage was lowered, and the pilot banked us in a tight turn over Cannes—blue sky one side, blue sea the other, our faith suspended between—and set us down at Nice–Côte d'Azur. Only ten minutes into town.

The taxi speeds along the Promenade des Anglais, braking sharply for the traffic lights. The Promenade, despite its name, seems to have become a six-lane shore-front motorway. But we walk the last minute of our journey, carrying our own bags, because our hotel—the Alfa—is in a pedestrianized section of the rue Masséna, a block north of the Promenade. We walk—*nous nous promenons*. There is something intensely intimate about French reflexive verbs like *se promener*, which make it seem as if we were we in a redoubled way, almost embracing one another or holding hands. Outside the hotel, pausing at the entrance, I say, "This is the place," and smile at Margot, my wife. Here we are. Again.

Two anniversaries are involved. It is twenty years, within a month or so, since we got married and caught the train on our first trip to Nice. We walked down the aisle of Beverley Minster, in East Yorkshire, and, after a few gulps of champagne and a bite of cake, were hustled off from the reception (which went merrily on without us) to catch the London train. And it is three years since I started La Conversation Française (Intermediate), a language class taught by Mme Monique Gaze on Wednesday evenings, during the academic year, at Goldsmiths' College, New Cross, London. I generally walk to the class through a decrepit section of the city. I thought that Margot and I might celebrate both anniversaries by going to Nice, where I could walk along the Promenade des Anglais.

I had picked the Alfa from a travel agent's brochure, attracted by its claim to be of modest size, comfortable, and family-run. Our room is at the front, on the *deuxième étage*. We can stand in the tall French windows and look out over a narrow balcony at the windows of the buildings opposite, at the shops and cafés below, and at people walking along the rue Masséna. Signs declare this to be a *Zone Piétonne*, where vehicles are permitted only when making deliveries between 6 and 11 a.m. I plump down on one of the beds, whose mattress sinks in a deep, sagging curve beneath me. This is a problem. I have "a back"—the modern malady—and a hard bed is the only thing. But for the moment I mustn't make a fuss about it. A letter from Antoine has been waiting for us, delivered by hand, and asks us to call up. We try to remember the name of the street on which Antoine and Lili lived when we stayed with them twenty years ago. At last, it comes to mind—rue Gubernatis, a street nearly in the old town, behind the market, in the direction of the port. Margot sees me putting on my jacket again, and says she will ring Antoine and Lili while I go for a stroll.

Tuesday: Antoine is sitting in the lobby waiting for us when we come from the breakfast room. Twenty years! Smiles, embraces, a multitude of questions, and answers that bring about further questions. So much catching up to do. Statements like "You don't look any different," which mean that we can see in each other's faces the chief characteristics of the persons we faintly remembered. And after a few minutes of this we all suddenly feel a need for air. Walking, we will be less choked by emotion, perhaps. We go out and walk along the Promenade, arm in arm, Antoine in the middle. Soon he and Margot are exchanging references, almost passwords, to the time when he and her father were best friends.

This friendship had been our chief reason for coming here the first time. Years before, Antoine had invited Margot's father and mother to visit him and Lili; but Margot's parents never came—we came instead. To seal this partial transfer of old ties to a new generation, Antoine and Lili's daughter Monique, who was studying English in England, had come to our wedding. Studying languages is at the root of the connection. Antoine speaks English in a heavily accented, Maurice Chevalier way, all the more redolent of roadsters, boaters, and girls in cloche hats for being at this moment, as we walk, concerned with the past. Antoine had been sent to England at eighteen to study the language in preparation for a career in hotelkeeping. He stayed in a boarding house in Ilford, on the northeastern outskirts of London; at meals there, he sat opposite a young Englishman who for two months did not speak a word, though he did nod to Antoine from time to time. Typical English, thought Antoine. Then, one day, the young man, whose name was Jim Speight, abruptly said to Antoine that if he wanted to learn English properly he ought to be staying with a family. The young man spoke in an accent that Antoine found curious; it was explained when the Englishman (who was roughly Antoine's age) said that he had just finished an engineering course and was going home to Hull, in Yorkshire. Why didn't Antoine come and stay with the Speight family?

And that was what Antoine did. For a year, he lived with the Speights, at 738 Holderness Road, Hull, paying for his keep, and fell into their ways. The house was always called Seven Three Eight. Jim was called Boy by his family. Boy's father was dead, but holding the reins were Uncle Leonard, who controlled the family finances, and Granny Speight, who ran Seven Three Eight. Antoine got to be friends with Boy's sisters, Nance and Helen, who were still at home, and he would have liked to become friends with a half sister, Margot, but for some reason she was rarely there. In Boy's company, he became well acquainted with the local pubs, sports grounds, and race tracks.

We walk along the inshore side of the Promenade, on a broad sidewalk. Six lanes of traffic, divided by a narrow median strip, pass between us and the even broader shorefront sidewalk, which is above the beach and overlooks the sea. Antoine is diverted from his ebullient memories of Seven Three Eight and Boy by the need to point out to us changes that have occurred since we were last here—like a new hotel housing a casino. We pass the Royal Hotel, where Antoine was once manager of the restaurant. He worked, he reminds us, in many such places—managed a hotel at Orly Airport for British European Airways, and ran a night club in Juan-les-Pins—but he is now retired, living with Lili and Monique and Monique's husband, Jean, and two granddaughters, in a large country house at Levens, fifteen miles north of Nice, in the foothills of the Alpes Maritimes. Antoine drives his granddaughters to school in Nice every morning, and Jean, who is the director of a large real-estate company, brings them home. As we walk, Antoine waves at many of the passersby, and they wave back. "*Salut!*" "*Ça va?*" We pass the front door of the Hotel Negresco just as a big Citroën pulls up and a tall, well-dressed man gets out. He greets Antoine, says hello to the doorman (who is in eighteenth-century costume), and enters the hotel, followed by two aides.

"Jacques Médecin," says Antoine, proudly. "Our mayor—and so was his father. He is also the Minister of Tourism of France."

"Why aren't *we* staying here?" Margot asks me. The Negresco is the *grand hôtel de luxe*—white dome, pink roofs, Art Nouveau décor—founded by the Rumanian entrepreneur Henri Negresco in 1912; once-crowned heads and film stars stayed there.

"Next time you will," Antoine says tactfully. "Boy and I used to go to the Four-in-Hand—or was it the Hare and Hounds? He showed me the form sheet he was keeping on the dogs at the local track." He sighs dramatically.

"The apartment on the rue Gubernatis," I say. "Was it opposite a bank?"

"Yes," says Antoine. "The bank is still there." One implication is that the bank might easily not have been there, such is the tide of modernization and redevelopment sweeping Nice.

"And that tennis match," I continue. "Do you remember taking us to it?"

"Ah, yes—it was in Cannes."

Our lives overlap. Our stay with Antoine and Lili for that one week is in Margot's and my memory as much as his stay in Hull is in Antoine's. Margot remembers the tiles in Lili's kitchen and the way she sliced tomatoes and sprinkled them with *herbes de Provence*. I remember the light coming in through the louvered shutters of our bedroom, and the rough linen sheets on our oak-headboarded bed. I remind Antoine (we are sitting in a café now, drinking coffee, with cars going by, palm fronds waving, shimmer of sea beyond), "The organizers had sold too many tickets for the match. There were fights between people who had tickets for the same seat. Gendarmes broke up the fights and sat down in the seats. People in the crowd outside were standing on the roofs of Rolls-Royces and sitting on the booms of construction cranes, which they swung overhead. Some were tearing down the fine privet hedge around the ground."

Margot says, "We also went to a restaurant near Saint-Paul."

"Les Oliviers, perhaps," says Antoine.

"That's the one," Margot says. "We ate outside. Roast lamb, grilled on an open fire, quite pink, with garlic. Stuffed tomatoes. Wine and then champagne. Some musicians walked in from the road, and one played on an accordion while the other sang. Tony cried because it was so beautiful."

· · ·

Margot and I spend the afternoon on the beach. We choose an uncrowded section of *la plage publique*. There are also *plages concédées*, with names like Miami, Ruhl, Bambou, Lido, and Sporting, where you pay for the privilege of having mats, chairs, and towels brought to you. The beach is made of flat stones—all shades of gray and a few slightly ocher. On the *plages concédées*, the attendants rearrange and flatten the stones with wooden rakes. The beach is fairly crowded, but only one or two people are swimming in the calm, blue, slightly antiseptic-looking sea.

Antoine has gone to meet Jean on a business errand; we have arranged to meet again tomorrow. Margot is painting a beachscape in watercolors—the French word *aquarelle* expresses the watery softness of the medium. She carries her supply of water for painting in a dried-milk carton. The people near us are mostly French; there are also a few elderly English and Americans, and a number of youngsters, college-student age, who appear to be American and Dutch. I doze for a while, making up for sleepless hours last night before I shifted my mattress to the floor. Waking up from my nap, I keep my eyes closed for a moment and put my hands down to feel the stones; then I pick up several and look at them. They are small, flat gray stones—but the one in my right hand has writing on it: careful, black, indelible felt-tip Spanish words, *Hoy mi ventana bebe el sol*. I roll over onto my right side and, where my hand had found the stone, find two more with messages on them. One says, *Como te llamas?* And the other, *Contempla la ciudad*. Three stones among millions of stones, and I knowing little Spanish—but it is hard to avoid the feeling that they were put here for me to find.

Leaving Margot painting, I make a reconnaissance of
the nearby section of the Promenade des Anglais. We
once lived on a street west of Central Park, in New York,
and the buildings here remind me of Central Park South,
though they are slightly lower, and have beach and sea
in place of the Park. Modern concrete-and-glass apartment buildings are set among older blocks of flats with
names like Le Milord, Le Roi Soleil, and Villa Saphir
(intimations of Babar). There are doctors' offices in
ground-floor suites, and flags of all nations flying from
the hotels—the Saudi-Arabian today at the Negresco.
There are other buildings done in Racquet Club Beaux-
Arts Classic; a few, like the Palais de la Méditerranée
Casino, are in thirties Odéon style, or basic Mussolini;
and a scattering of late-nineteenth-century villas have
outcropping conservatories and balconies and sundry
rococo flourishes. The mall dividing the highway is
planted with palms and bougainvillea. The shorefront
road that starts about half a mile to the east below the
Mont aux Morts, with its castle remains and cemetery,
is called Quai des Etats-Unis, but at the Jardin Albert Iᵉʳ
(built over the tunnel through which the River Paillon
reaches the sea) the road becomes the Promenade des
Anglais. The slice of it on which one walks next to the
sea—what in English seaside resorts would be called
the front—is generally thirty feet wide, is paved with a
crushed-raspberry-colored asphalt, and is flanked by a
wall that drops ten feet to the beach. Along the pavement
are placed green steel chairs and white wooden benches
on which one can sit with one's feet comfortably resting
on the rail that runs along the edge of the wall. But not
all of the crushed-raspberry *trottoir* is for promenading.
Parts of it are given over to car parking, and mopeds and

motorcycles operated by nonchalant youths ignore the signs forbidding them access and weave in and out among the strolling people—some of whom raise their fists and shout at the riders *"Imbécile!"* or *"Drug addicte!"*

I walk for a little way and then flop down in one of the chairs. With hills close behind it, the city squats along the curve of the Baie des Anges—the Bay of Angels —with Cap d'Etretat to the west and, to the east, Cap Ferrat (beyond which lie Monte Carlo and Menton). Today, the blue-and-white distinctness of Mediterranean light is blurred by petroleum haze. The sea looks clean but slightly dead, with no visible seaweed or marine life; more pigeons than seagulls fly over the beach. But fortunately some of the noise and smell of traffic is wafted off inland by a light onshore breeze. On the beach, sunbathers are taking the sun seriously; women of all ages conduct public beauty treatments on themselves, rubbing oils and lotions on and off, and glancing up from these narcissistic exercises only to stare at anyone who looks like venturing, bizarrely, into the water. A number of these sunbathers, both middle-aged and *en fleur*, are dressed only in the bottom halves of their bikinis and lie on their backs, sunny-side up. Although a few energetic spirits are paddling kayaks or pedaling *pédalo* catamarans a yard or so out to sea, serious activity on the beach is confined to various venders, carrying wicker panniers and crying their wares. A woman with bulky baskets suspended from her shoulders clatters over the stones, which click and slither beneath her feet; she is selling pralines and copies of *Nice-Matin*, the local paper. A young man calls out, *"Glaces, chocolat, bière, soda!"* and then, *"Orangina, Coca-Cola, bière, Schweppessssssss!"*

When I return from my small exploration, Margot says, "Do you remember, I bought a bikini and lost the top half of it out of my bag while we were walking back from the beach?"

"So you were the one who invented this topless thing?"

"I think the Germans did. Anyway, I had to use the top of my old black one."

"The black and tans."

And a little later I remember: "The haircut."

"It was the best haircut you ever had."

I wonder if I could find that barbershop again. Some things don't come back, though one is aware of them, almost—aware that one ought to be able to recall whether he did such-and-such but can't.

Margot takes off some clothes to reveal a one-piece swimsuit. She walks down to the water and plunges in. Along the entire beach, as far as I can see in either direction, only one other person is in the water.

When she is getting dry, she says, "Frenchmen do have hairy legs. Aunt Helen always said they did."

Of my wife's father's three sisters, Nance died giving birth to a daughter; Margot (after whom my wife was named) disappeared from family view; and Helen lived for many years with her second husband, Leon (a Polish Army officer who came to England during the war), in Pau, on the French side of the Pyrénées. In the twenties, Helen was often here in Nice. According to Dien Creeft, a Dutch woman we met in Amsterdam, later on our honeymoon, she and Helen once slept on the Nice beach all night in their ocelot coats. And that was earlier in the year than the present month of June—which was then considered unchic and out of season. *Tourisme d'été* was only just beginning.

The Alfa serves no meals except breakfast. Our *demi-pension* arrangement is subcontracted to a restaurant, Le Grillon, around the corner on the rue Halévy, where we may eat the prix-fixe, twenty-two-franc three-course dinner without any money changing hands—though we pay for extra dishes and for drinks. In fact, since we invariably pay for wine, we generally feel that we might as well stretch out in other directions, à la carte. Margot admires tripes niçoise. I eat tarts and crêpes galore. Our only doubt is whether our affability will survive our being thrown at each other in this way, by eating meals in restaurants—indeed, by being on holiday. At home, children prevent us from being so much alone. Here we have waves of affection and bouts of grumpiness, emanating from the feeling that we are packaged together. It seems wrong to read while eating, in a public place, as we do in our own kitchen, though such books as my phrase book and the Michelin Guide Vert to the Côte d'Azur lie on the checked Le Grillon tablecloth. And we do read them under the pretense of consulting them. Margot has also brought along a copy of G. M. Trevelyan's *Garibaldi and the Thousand*, and this—after several meals of amicable *en vacances* conversation between us —has begun to compete successfully with me for her attention. (Garibaldi was born in Nice in 1807.)

I say, between forkfuls of spaghetti, "The Promenade des Anglais has three stars in the Michelin guide. *'Jusqu'en 1820, la côte, à cet endroit, était d'accès difficile. Vers cette époque, la colonie anglaise, nombreuse depuis le 18ᵉ siècle, prit à sa charge l'établissement du sentier riverain qui est à l'origine de la voie actuelle et qui lui a donné son nom.'*"

"What's a *sentier riverain*?" Margot asks.

"Strictly, a riverside path, but I imagine they mean a waterside path in this case," I reply after consulting my pocket dictionary.

"Tell me more."

"*Demain.*"

Wednesday: Old guidebooks mention an "English library." According to a late-nineteenth-century Baedeker I have, this library was in the Crédit Lyonnais building, but it is there no longer. Antoine thinks that it may be somewhere near the English church, which is on the rue de la Buffa. Today, I went looking for it, but before doing so I decided to have a conversation about the soft bed with the Alfa's *patron.* My difficulties with it are combined with those arising from our position at the front of the hotel, overlooking the picturesque *Zone Piétonne.* There, as it has transpired, people walk and talk each night until 3 a.m., and then the café proprietors (one of whom owns an irritable German shepherd) put their chairs and tables away—the sounds of metal scraping over the paving, chairs clattering together —and next a number of small-hours hooligans take advantage of the empty street to rocket through it on their motorcycles. All this accounts for my haggard looks this morning. The Alfa's *patron* is about my age, in the mid-torrent of life—a genial fellow, I thought. But now the honor of his hotel appears to be at stake. *No one* has ever complained about a mattress before. The French like them. The Swedes like them. So do the Japanese. *There are no harder beds in the hotel.* This is not, of course, the Negresco. But, monsieur . . .

I explain, *aussi en français,* that the problem is more common than he imagines. *Une condition humaine.*

Most English hotels can provide a piece of plywood for those who need such extra support under their mattresses. I tell the *patron* that I sleep on a hard bed at home and, without something to stiffen his soft bed, will not sleep at all. What a way to enjoy Nice!

Great Gallic shrugs. Well, he will look and see. There is no plywood in the hotel, but perhaps . . . he will see.

Holy Trinity, the English church, two blocks inland from the Promenade, has a graveyard with numerous nineteenth-century tombstones commemorating those English who died here, invalid consumptives or fever-stricken colonials on their way to or from the Indies. "To the memory of Colonel Bentham Sandwith, Bombay Light Cavalry, died at Cannes 1850." "In memory of Rev. H. F. Lyte, author of 'Abide with me: fast falls the eventide.' " The graveyard is overgrown rather than overcrowded. Marguerites, geraniums, and lilies flower beneath tangled shrubbery. A black cat stalks through tall, dark-green, Rousseau-like grass. High, nondescript apartment buildings hem in the funereal plot on three sides, and in the basement of one, fronting the rue de France, is what is now called the English-American Library—a single long room lined with dark shelves, and with a few tables and chairs where members may sit and read papers and magazines. Here I introduce myself to Mr. A. Wilner, the library secretary. A dapper elderly gentleman, he tells me that until his retirement he worked for Barclays Bank in Nice. (Somerset Maugham was a customer.) Mr. Wilner also tells me that there are fewer English in Nice than there were before the war; the loss is noticeable in winter. Now Nice has more tourists, fewer foreign winter residents. It is a much bigger city. The French retire here. The last British consul left Nice in January 1976 and is now in Marseilles.

I poke around in the library, whose shelves hold the collected works of Georgette Heyer and Mazo de la Roche. (Maugham is in a special cabinet.) I find accounts in various books of the coming of the English in the mid-eighteenth century to this sleepy Mediterranean port—an ancient Greek settlement named after Nike, the goddess of victory. The English were drawn southward, despite brigands and cold in the mountains, by such attractions as the university and school of medicine at Montpellier. From there, they traveled east to Nice, which was then part of the Kingdom of Sardinia, and where they found cheap living in a good climate. No proper road existed along the coast; feluccas carried the travelers from Marseilles or Antibes. An early publicist of Nice's advantages was Smollett, who came here in 1763 for a pulmonary disorder. He bathed every day, even in winter. He liked the "serene sky," the "not unwholesome" water, the readily procurable good food, and the fact that fogs were unknown. In Nice, he said, "I have breathed more freely than I have done for some years, and my spirits have been more alert." Soon the English were building villas; they distributed Bibles and took long walks. Although there was an English exodus during the French Revolution and the Napoleonic Wars, when the Comté de Nice was occupied by the French, the English returned in 1814, when Nice was handed back to the House of Savoy.

The founder of the Promenade des Anglais arrived in 1822. I admit to a slight *frisson* of alma-mater pride on reading that Lewis Way was, as I am, a former member of Merton College, Oxford. He became both a minister and a barrister, and then, at the age of thirty-two, inherited three hundred thousand pounds. He decided to throw up the law, and set forth to convert the Jews to Christianity and restore Palestine to them. Nice was to be his base for approaching the Jews of the Mediterranean coast with this scheme. He brought his family overland, while dispatching the children's ponies, Mrs. Way's piano, and their daughter Drusilla's harp by sea. In Nice, Way the philanthropist was soon known as Louis d'Or. "People are plaguing Lewis for money," Mrs. Way wrote to her mother. "He has advanced £150 to one, and made an allowance to another for 3 or 4 years." Lewis Way found in Nice an impoverished government and people. The citrus crop had failed. In order to help the unemployed peasants, who had flocked into the city, and at the same time benefit the English residents, who liked taking walks by the sea, Way organized charity drives and with his own funds paid for the construction of *le sentier riverain*. When he left Nice, in 1824, a path had been built, two yards wide, westward from the mouth of the Paillon as far as the rue Meyerbeer—close to where, on the Promenade, the Hotel Westminster now stands.

And so, although his conversion plans came to nothing, Way's way became a success; it was gradually lengthened, widened, and improved. In 1844, La Strada del Littorale was officially renamed the Promenade des Anglais. By that time, it had reached the Quartier Baumettes, near the Boulevard Carlone. In 1856, it arrived at the Magnan Torrent, which is possibly a torrent in comparison with the Paillon, a stream generally described in the guidebooks as insignificant. In summer, the Paillon's wide, stony bed is dry, save for a trickle down the middle. (However, a note from Antoine: "In the old days, the Niçoises did their washing in what there was of the Paillon, and would leave their laundry to dry on the flat stones of the riverbed. After a heavy rain in the mountains, the Paillon would come down like a small Niagara, and a man on horseback would gallop ahead of the waterfall, shouting—in the Nice dialect—'*Paillon ven! Paillon ven!*' He was on the city payroll.")

In 1860, when a plebiscite was held and Nice rejoined France, there were more improvements on the Promenade: horses, carriages, and walkers were disentangled; people on foot were given a wide pedestrian way, lined with trees; palms were planted. At this time, says the *Histoire de Nice*, edited by Maurice Bordes, the Promenade was the symbol of the town and of "*sa vie de saison.*" Yet it was not entirely urban: shepherds and their dogs, if not their sheep, were seen on it. In 1895, according to Baedeker's guide for that year, the Promenade had just been prolonged to the western suburb of Californie. In 1931, the Duke of Connaught opened a further enlargement of the Promenade. In 1940, under the Vichy regime, the unemployed were once again set to work on it.

Walking back to the beach, to join Margot, I am twice approached for money. Many people in Nice are retired or are on holiday or simply at leisure, and a large number of layabouts are occupied in making them feel guilty about their good fortune and in removing any spare cash they have on them. Panhandlers and mendicants abound. The outstretched hand is everywhere. North African peddlers hawk jewelry and leather goods. Gypsy women hold out to you their shawl-swaddled infants. Tough local scroungers and young international hippies team up for intimidating effect. Others simply stick out their palms and mumble a need for alms. The mothers have their babies, and the hippies have one another—some have found, apparently, that working in pairs softens up the potentially charitable. Many of these beggars work both the Promenade des Anglais and the pavement cafés on the rue Masséna, where the open palm suddenly appears as you are about to bite into a pizza or take a sip of Ricard. Along the Promenade, there are gangs of beggars, but this tends to be counter-productive: if you gave to one, wouldn't you have to give to all? And you give more readily to those who make some sort of return. A young couple with guitars do a round of the little restaurants singing songs of the "Tomorrow Doesn't Matter" / "La Vie en Rose" kind—the troubadour tradition. A fire-eater hangs out on the Promenade and now and then makes sorties onto the streets between it and the rue Masséna, shooting forth a jet of blazing petroleum vapor from his mouth while members of his motley entourage collect francs from passersby and people sitting in nearby cafés. After night-fall, the coming of this band is heralded by the sudden glow of the ejected fireball; the group's passage through an area is indicated by a long-lingering smell of kerosene. (Antoine, after a day or so, gave me the words one ought to have at one's disposal in Nice, as I heard him say to one of the child-carrying gypsy women, *"Non, j'ai donné déjà aujourd'hui, madame."* The statement that one had already made one's daily charitable gift lets one off the hook.)

At dinner at Le Grillon, after we have been serenaded by the two young guitarists, Margot tells me about Garibaldi. At the age of fifteen, he and several friends ran away from Nice by boat, but they were caught off

Monaco and brought home. A long time later, he declared, according to Trevelyan, "It gives me joy to bring to mind the young men of Nice: agile, strong, brave, splendid social and military material, but unfortunately led on the wrong path, first by the priests, then by depravity brought in from foreign parts, which has turned the beautiful Cimele of the Romans into the cosmopolitan seat of all that is corrupt." Something here of the feelings of a local when faced with tourism, I suspect.

After eating, we stroll along the Promenade. I whistle snatches from the between-the-wars song "The Man Who Broke the Bank at Monte Carlo": "As I walk along the Bois de Boulogne, / With an independent air, / All the people stare . . ." In a little while, we sit down in two chairs on the seaward edge of the Promenade, backs to the traffic, and regard the sea, the beach, and the lights of the Promenade and its extensions curving with the bay around us. There is a magic moment around nine-thirty, as the lights come on along the whole length of the Promenade, and sky and sea go dark together. A dot of bright light appears over the sea. Is it a planet or a plane coming in to land? The darkening of the slate-colored sea makes the small fringe of surf seem whiter; it arrives, gleaming, on the yard or so of wet shingle from which the tide has withdrawn—as much as it ever does. The light of the Promenade reflected in the water is a sort of white shadow that runs in, preceding the surf's splashy face. High on the façades of the more important buildings, big neon names light up: NEGRESCO. RUHL. WESTMINSTER. From Cap Ferrat, to the east, the lighthouse flashes regularly every three seconds. From Cap d'Antibes, westward, a light emits two long blinks in an occulting cycle, three seconds and seven seconds apart. On the beach in front of us, a few people are trying to skip stones. A young couple walk down to the water's edge and stand looking out; she wears a shiny black raincoat. Twenty years ago, Margot had a coat like that. The girl, black-haired, looks like Margot then. The young man takes his shoes off and wades. It is as if we were sitting watching ourselves. Time has stopped, or circled back on itself. But the Antibes light keeps flashing, the blink followed by first a short, then a long, dark interval.

Thursday: Driving with Antoine eastward on the Moyenne Corniche—up behind Villefranche, behind the skyscrapers of Monaco, to join the new motorway into Italy. Market day in Ventimiglia. It takes us a while to find a parking space, and probably we burn in fuel what Antoine saves on the three bottles of Ricard—the duty-free quota—he buys here because it is cheaper than in France. Then we drive back across the border to Menton, where Antoine was born. Today would have been his mother's birthday, if she were alive, and up on the hill overlooking the town and the harbor we visit the Trabuquet cemetery, where Antoine installs in a vase on the family plot a bunch of gladioli brought from the Nice market. The water tap is locked, and Antoine fills his vase with water from an empty vase on a nearby grave. He looks at the headstone, with the surname LANTERI and the various Christian names underneath; there is room for him. Along each side of the path are graves: more English consumptives, naval men and colonials, and soldiers of the First World War who died in hospital here. Several ranks of graves belong to French soldiers from African territories, such as Chad and Mauritania, who died, so their headstones say, *Pour la Patrie*, but a long way from home.

We walk in the old part of Menton and lunch at a splendid restaurant on the Quai Bonaparte: La Belle Escale. We sit outside, with a view of the harbor. At the suggestion of the *patronne*, I have grilled *loup de mer*, which is sea bass, and regret it only when I get the bill; it is my treat. We take the lower road back to Nice, past a restaurant where, Margot and I remember as we catch sight of it, we lunched with Antoine twenty years ago. We pass through Roquebrune, with its small stone "V" memorial to the English *hivernant* Sir Winston Churchill. As we go by the Monte Carlo casinos, Antoine remembers that he and Margot's father used to play a lot of vingt-et-un, or blackjack, under its English name of pontoon. "Pontoon and bust!" says Antoine. He has memories of coming in late with Boy and making the long climb up the squeaky stairs of Seven Three Eight to the attic room they shared. The trouble with coming in late in winter was having no hot-water bottle when you needed it most. Boy had a whippet. Antoine ate fish and chips with gusto and liked British beer. And then there was Boy's half sister, Margot, seen infrequently but much admired by Antoine. What ever happened to her? My wife has a faint recollection that Margot went to Argentina and was never in touch with the family again.

Antoine sets us down near the Jardin Albert Ier, and we arrange to see him again on Sunday, for a day with his family. We thank him. He is *très gentil*—the word means kind but has the extra overtones to the English of gentle and gentleman.

"Ah," says Antoine, "as you know, I would have liked to do this for Boy and Betty"—Margot's mother—"but they would never come here. So I do it for you."

At the hotel, I have a problem requiring diplomacy. Yesterday, the proprietor found me two planks, which helped a great deal—the bed was no longer a soft pit of discomfort, compelling insomnia. However, the *Zone Piétonne* remains a small-hours bedlam. Now that I have my *planches*, I feel churlish in presenting the proprietor with a further difficulty, but it is (I say to him when I meet him in the entrance hall) important that we move to a quieter room—perhaps one at the back of the hotel. I have done my research in dictionary and phrase book. I give him a graphic description of noises in the rue Masséna at 3 a.m. The *patron* grips the reception desk as I go through the list of aural horrors; *le chien méchant* and a loudly rendered *"Rowf, rowf, rowf!"* really clinch it. The *patron* says, resignedly (a party of Swedes has stopped to listen), that the room across the hall from our present room is free. We may move into it. I tell him, happily, that I will carry over my planks myself. You can just about see him thinking, *Mon Dieu, ces anglais . . .*

Friday: Margot and I aren't talking today. Whose fault is it? Something I said? Something I didn't say? Something chemical, or alchemical, or the stars? She goes off to paint on the beach, and I go to the library, where I read how Napoleon improved the roads and, consequently, the English could reach the Riviera in less than a fortnight. But despite the natives' custom of calling all foreigners "English" it wasn't just the English who came. All the royal families of Europe turned up in Nice, and so did statesmen like Talleyrand and Metternich, and such men of letters as Alexandre Dumas, Robert Louis Stevenson, and Guy de Maupassant, who had *"quelques liaisons"* here. Offenbach wintered in Nice. Berlioz lodged in rooms in Les Ponchettes, a low terrace of buildings between the market and the Quai des Etats-Unis. "There," he said, "I live alone, I write, I sing. I believe in God." He also took walks on the rocks overlooking the sea, and on one such stroll he was arrested; he was thought to be an accomplice of revolutionaries, and was immediately asked to leave Nice. Paganini, although he was very rich, lived parsimoniously in a third-floor room on the rue de Préfecture, and he died there, in May 1840, having refused the last rites of the Church; he was denied burial in consecrated ground. Friedrich Nietzsche, then a professor at Basel, spent part of five winters here, from 1883 to 1888, writing *Beyond Good and Evil.* An earth tremor on February 23, 1887, frightened many into leaving town, but Nietzsche stayed put. Berthe Morisot painted in Nice, as did Rosa Bonheur, who lived in the Villa Africaine, on the Promenade des Anglais, with her friend Mlle Nica—also a painter—and numerous animals, including sheep and goats. Dressed in velvet pantaloons and a circus lion-tamer's blouse, Rosa Bonheur would stride along the Promenade sporting the ribbon of the Légion d'Honneur.

Many of the great villas that rose along the Promenade during the nineteenth century were occupied by Russians. The Tsar and Tsarina used to arrive by sea, with a Russian naval flotilla in attendance. The Grand Duke Constantine stayed in the Maison Dalmas; and at the Villa Romanoff, also on the Promenade, dwelt the Bashkirtseff family—one member of which, Marie, was a young diarist and consumptive who wrote and wrote under the nom de plume of Moussia. (Eighty-four volumes of her diary, covering the years 1873–84, are in the Bibliothèque Nationale, Paris.) She used to ride along the Promenade in a basket cart, lined with white bearskins, pulled by two matching ponies. She wrote come-hither letters to Maupassant. In her highly emotional journals, she wrote about getting up to watch the sunrise over the coastal mountains, "clearly etoned against the blue sky—a soft vaporous blue," and about "the nights when the moon cuts a swath in the sea, like a fish with diamond scales." She was the object of a literary cult in France, but in England one reviewer wrote, "Mademoiselle Bashkirtseff attracts and repels alternatively, and perhaps repels as much as she attracts." A more recent Russian memoirist, Vladimir Nabokov, recalls in *Speak, Memory* the occasion when his invalid grandfather was being rolled along the Promenade des Anglais in his wheelchair and mistook his attendant for a long-deceased colleague in the Russian Cabinet. The Russian Revolution affected Nice badly. One observer there, a journalist named Herbert Adams Gibbons, noted, "Before the end of the war, the center of the Russian colony was a soup kitchen on a side street, presided over by princesses . . ."

I climb forth from the dimly lit cellar and go out to the Promenade for lunch in the sun. I sit on the terrace of a café next to the Palais de la Méditerranée, the casino that Frank Jay Gould, the American millionaire, built in 1929. The terrace is screened with glass, like most such places along the Promenade, to keep out traffic noise and fumes. My table is one of the few that are unshaded by umbrellas, but it is fine to sit here dipping into an old book I have borrowed from the library, drinking a beer, and watching people walk by. I write a poem:

En plein soleil, sans parapluie,
Parmi les pigeons du Casino,
Je bois un Kronenbourg
Et lis
Un livre d'autrefois.

I spend the afternoon back in the library. It seems that the railway made a great change in Nice. Trains reached Toulon about 1855 and Nice in 1864: a day and a night's journey from England. The age of milords ended. Nice was accessible to the middle classes. By 1880, ten big hotels had been built, including, on the Promenade, the Victoria (now the West End), the Hôtel de Luxembourg, and the Hôtel des Anglais, all of which closed "out of season"; that is, in summer. The Blue Train—the Calais–Paris–Nice express—made its first run in December 1883, with only ten passengers and a valet in each blue-and-gold-liveried *wagon-lit.* To welcome the new train service, Nice put on a *grande exposition,* and various improvements were undertaken: the infamous sewers that emptied into the sea opposite the hotels and villas of the Promenade were rebuilt and redirected; the Place Masséna, over the mouth of the Paillon, was enlarged, and a municipal casino opened there to lure gamblers from Monte Carlo, a new rival. In the propaganda war that took place at the time, Nice portrayed Monte Carlo as a highly dissolute spot, where visitors often committed suicide after losing at roulette. Monte Carlo published its death records to counter these slurs, and engineered press reports that Nice was in the grip of a cholera epidemic.

It helped that Her Britannic Majesty liked Nice. Queen Victoria used to stay in the suburb of Cimiez, and often drove around town in her little donkey cart, preceded by a *piqueur* who called out, "*La Reine passe!*" Her eldest son, later Edward VII, generally lodged on the Promenade under the incognito of Baron Renfrew and tried to stay out of Mama's way. Oscar Wilde, shortly after being released from jail, saw the Prince of Wales one day and raised his hat as the Prince drove along the Promenade. Edward failed to recognize Wilde, and a companion said, "That was Oscar Wilde." So the Prince had his carriage turn back and, passing Wilde again, raised his hat and bowed to him.

In the train posters of the nineteen-twenties, elegant men and women are shown in the corridors of the Blue Train, leaning against the window rails or perching on little fold-down seats as the coast goes by outside, with its capes and bays. The passengers look so calm and collected. As for me, I was so very excited getting off our train in Nice twenty years ago that I left my briefcase in the overhead rack. It went off with half a book manuscript in it. I walked daily from the rue Gubernatis to the police station and the railway station to see if it had been recovered. It was, in fact, recovered at Ventimiglia, and was shipped, courtesy of various European railways, to us in Amsterdam, several weeks later.

Margot and I have regained our companionability this evening. It helps to see other couples fighting. On the rue Masséna, a woman runs from a man, saying distractedly, "*C'est fini—fini!*" The existential freedom of holidays is hard to cope with, and it seems a good idea to impose on this nerve-racking flux a structure of errands, research, painting, shopping, sunbathing—setting a time for each. Presumably, it is this so-much-time-to-kill vacuum that gambling fills, besides satisfying an urge that many people have. I do not, unless sometimes while

I'm racing a sailboat, when I suddenly feel bound to tack on a hunch or a flier. The idea of losing even small sums of money horrifies me—far more than the prospect of sudden riches gives me delight. But, since casinos are part of Nice, Margot and I drop into the Palais de la Méditerranée after dinner, thinking that it may be more agreeable than the newer Ruhl Casino. (Had we but known it, the Ruhl Casino and the Palais were about to be fought over, in what was apparently a gangland war to control Riviera casinos, and in this struggle—with murders, disappearances, vast tax debts, great losses, and great wins—both the Ruhl and the Palais de la Méditerranée were to founder.) For a while, we watch a low-stakes game of chance in a ground-floor room, and then we climb the grandiose staircase in search of baccarat and roulette: the green felt, the shaded lights, women in evening dress, a few piles of chips getting larger while the rest are raked away. An official blocks our path: "*Passeport? Carte d'identité?*" Our passports are at the hotel; the English do not carry identity cards. *Quel dommage*, but there is no entry without them; it has something to do with a list the casino keeps, either of those whom the casino does not trust to pay up or of those who have asked to be barred because their will power has its ups and downs.

Lady Polwarth, in Nice in the seventeen-seventies with her consumptive husband, met Lady Drogheda— "the best and most sensible person, and I am sorry to think that she is married to a whimsical Irishman, who has half ruined himself by gaming and could not help losing two hundred pounds, even here." Kenneth Clark writes, in *The Romantic Rebellion*, "When I was young I spent a good deal of time walking up and down the Promenade des Anglais at Nice, waiting for my father to emerge, flushed and victorious—as he always was—from the Casino." Those waits gave Clark the chance to observe various buildings in what he called "that strip of architectural monstrosities," including the Villa Neptune, whose façade was covered with sculptured figures that "heaved and wriggled with tropical abundance"; two of the caryatids supporting the principal window were by Rodin. In the first half of this century, one of Nice's several casinos, resembling a miniature Santa Sophia, stood on a little pier, the Jetée Promenade, near the mouth of the Paillon. The Germans made the Promenade des Anglais off limits during the Second World War. They built a concrete wall at the end of every street leading to it. Antoine says, "On August 25, 1944, all the Niçois ran over the walls to see if our beloved Promenade was still there. Yes, it was, but no more Jetée Promenade—the Germans had destroyed it."

Saturday: Antoine drives us to his home in the Alpes Maritimes foothills. It is a large, low house—a *bastide*, it is called—surrounded by a stone wall and overlooking olive groves and fields. Levens sits on a nearby hilltop. Antoine's son-in-law, Jean—whose name is pronounced "Jong," in the local fashion—is already at work in the outdoor kitchen by the swimming pool, preparing pizza dough, chopping mushrooms, making a sauce for the fish, which is dorado. Jean and his father own and manage several apartment houses, which are to the present what hotels were to the last century. Jean is also a great cook. The meal, which takes place on the terrace, lasts a good part of the afternoon. We eat and drink and talk. At one point, Lili says, "*Ah—Tony parle bien français!*" I glow with pleasure at this kindly judgment—some idiom learned one evening in darkest New Cross has just come to me, at the perfect moment, on the wings of wine and out of the exaltation of well-being. *Merci, Mme Gaze.* Afterward, to walk off some of the physical effects of this repast, Margot and I climb into the little nearby mountains—two hours of rambling among the rocks, sage, and maquis. We walk along paths that with rain might be small torrents. And after we return to the house Antoine and Margot explore Seven Three Eight once again, one memory provoking another.

When Antoine has driven us back, he sets us down in the Place Masséna. We say goodbye and express our thanks with a blitheness, even a brevity, that is camouflage for our feelings that we will probably never see Antoine again. Of course, we say openly that we will always remember this visit and his kindness. Antoine, similarly affected, says he will come to London to see us in the fall. But he will not.

Sunday: I slept log-like in the room at the rear of the hotel, *avec mes planches sous le matelas.*

And this is it, the last full day. What am I here for? *Contempla la ciudad.* Shortly after breakfast, I set off to walk the length of the seafront. I proceed to the eastern end of the Quai des Etats-Unis, under the castle, on its crag, and start my promenade, sauntering westward with an independent air, exchanging glances of casual curiosity with the people I pass. One purpose of promenading is to take deep breaths in the open while one sees and is seen. It is a form of delight in the existence, or, at least, the appearance, of other human beings —and in one's own existence. The morning is radiant. I stride past Les Ponchettes, the terrace of flat-roofed houses that wall off the market from the esplanade. I pause to admire the ornamental planting in the Jardin

Albert Ier—palms, pepper trees, aloes, laurels, and myrtles —and the benches, railings, and notices forbidding walking on the grass. Here is the Monument du Centenaire, put up in 1892 to commemorate the one-hundredth anniversary of the first conjunction of Nice and France: a maternal figure embracing a younger woman—France the mother, Nice the daughter.

At the Jardin, the Quai becomes the Promenade, whose continued attribution to the English appears unthreatened by the Middle Eastern flags flying from hotel flagstaffs and the OPEC money that is said to be fueling the casinos. I see people I have seen during the past few days, strolling or taking it easy. The fire-eater and some of his entourage are stretched out on the beach; he undoubtedly needs the fresh air. In front of the white domes and faded pink roofs of the Negresco, a woman—my wife—is looking out to sea, painting. How attractive she looks, how absorbed in what she is doing! Meanwhile, the German and Dutch tour buses are trundling by, and planes are taking off from the airport. A length of seawall is being rebuilt, and for a quarter of a mile there are many trucks and loading machines, much dust and noise, and many signs saying NICOLETTI, the construction firm responsible. Toward the end of the Promenade, after some four miles, I begin to think of food: salade niçoise, tripes niçoise, supion (baby cuttlefish) à la niçoise, ratatouille à la niçoise, Nice biscuits, Garibaldi biscuits, Victoria sponge, Battenberg cake. A motor caravan with British license plates is parked by the curb, and through one window I can see next to the gas stove a tin of Heinz tomato soup.

But the terrain where the Promenade actually ends is not uncharming. A newly grassed hill obscures a pumping works by the shore, and the roadway, renamed the

Promenade Edouard Corniglion-Molinier, swings inland past the airport. At the end of the Promenade des Anglais, a little curved breakwater forms a small harbor, where skiffs and small fishing boats are moored. Here, on a strip of sand and gravel, several men are playing *boules* (or, as it is generally called in these parts, *pétanque*), taking turns at throwing, and then huddling over the *boules* to decide, with much discussion, who is closer. Presumably, therefrom came our bowls and bowling. And here, possibly because I have done what I set out to do and need a new challenge, I decide that on the way back I will go and look on the beach for those three stones with Spanish writing on them. It is as if I wanted to prepare a memory for the future. I will say to Margot if we come here in perhaps another twenty years' time, "Do you remember those stones on the beach with the Spanish words on them? Do you remember how, on the day before we left, I went looking for them but didn't find them?"

THE CORACLE, EUSTACE,

AND THE RIVER

we traveled on the same ship across the Atlantic, and for the period that Mike ran the London bureau of his New Zealand newspaper, we met them quite often. When they went home, we exchanged Christmas greetings most years and gave each other news of jobs, homes, and children. Margie taught school and Mike became the general manager of his Wellington paper. This letter said that they would be in England for a week. When they arrived, Margot invited them to dinner at our house in Greenwich, in southeast London, on May 30. Margot said to me: "I've told them to come early enough so we can walk in the park."

May 30 was also the date of an annular eclipse of the sun, visible (so my desk diary informed me) as a partial eclipse in various parts of the world from the Hawaiian Islands to Algeria; it would be seen in the British Isles in early evening. The Robsons beat the rush hour out of town in time for tea, and then we set off for the park to witness the shadowing of the sun by the moon, giving ourselves as a turn-around point one of the riverside pubs. The park is five minutes from our house, and I walk in it nearly every day with our springer spaniel, Daisy. It is beautiful, the result of French classical landscape design and English terrain and three centuries of growth, decay, and care. Daisy also finds it interesting, liking her daily opportunity to send squirrels scooting up the ancient Spanish chestnuts and her chance to spring over park benches. She made forays now in the direction of the Old Observatory, which stands on top of a steep escarpment and provides a fine prospect of London. I suggested we make the climb, to view the eclipse and the city, but Margot and the Robsons were eager to steer a course across the park, toward the boating pond and the gate, at the eastern end of the National Maritime

Museum, which would allow us to walk most directly to the river. This way would also lead us to the Greenwich Meridian, zero degrees, from which longitudinal distance round the earth has been measured since 1884 for the convenience of mariners and accurate timekeeping, and whose centenary this year was marked by a white stripe painted through the park on the grass, joining the brass strips that here and there regularly denote the division of the world into zones east and west of Greenwich. Visitors like to stand on the spot where the meridian is marked at the Old Observatory with their feet apart, one in each zone.

The light was diminishing as we approached the boating pond, a concreted depression at whose center a flotilla of aluminum hire canoes was moored for the night. A man appeared from behind a tree, clutching a camera. Several other people were just visible by the pond in the temporary twilight. The camera seemed to be trained on me and then on Daisy, who, ears swinging near the ground, was lolloping toward a round black object that lay near the pond, looking like an umbrella without its handle or a huge truncated toadstool. As I got closer to it, it had more of the appearance of a small tar-and-canvas geodesic dome, but such a structure would not seem to have called for the presence of the man with the camera, whom I had by now recognized as Piet van der Merwe, a good friend and an officer at the Maritime Museum. On the grass next to the black shape stood a two-liter brown plastic bottle of Whitbread Bitter. With a polite request to Daisy, who was sniffing at the thing, to stand aside, I lifted it and turned it over on the grass. It sat like a big black basket, lined with a lattice of green-painted laths, a pine thwart spanning it across the diameter. Though I had never seen such an object before,

The Coracle, Eustace, and the River

I knew what it was. Several fluid ounces of Celtic and possibly old British blood run in my veins. I said, "Golly,
a coracle." Margot said to me, "Yes, happy birthday."

A demonstration was in order and was provided by a
colleague of Piet's, a young woman who had experience
in handling coracles. My coracle was picked up easily
and launched at the pond edge. Unlike most other boats
I have owned, when put in, it did not leak a drop. The
young woman from the museum stepped gently into the
middle of the craft, while hanging onto the concrete rim
of the pond. The paddle looked like a large wooden
spade of the sort children use at the seaside, and with this
she sculled skillfully away, making a sort of figure-eight
motion in the water out in front of the coracle. Then she
turned and came back in. Piet tried it next; getting in
could clearly be difficult—water lapped over the rim at
the front and then, as Piet moved the other way, at the
back. He sat down quickly. When he had returned from
a short trial voyage, we lifted the coracle out, decanted
several pints of water, and then relaunched it. It was
now the new owner's turn. I understood from what I'd
seen that the art of embarkation involved counteracting
the coracle's inherent tendency to slip sideways if given
half a chance, leaving the would-be occupant in the
notorious, irremediable situation of being stretched
further and further between sea and shore—until the
splash. I negotiated that part of the operation safely and
seated myself gently. Suddenly the coracle rocked. Daisy
had jumped into it to join me. I pushed off, while Daisy
sat by my left knee, staring forward as if on lookout.
First, I tried an orthodox canoe-paddling stroke on one
side, then the other, and the coracle whirled round, clock-
wise, then widdershins. Next, I attempted to emulate the
motion the young museum woman had made over the

bows, slicing the water from side to side, and this finally began to pull the coracle forward, more or less in the intended direction. In a conventional rowboat, Daisy usually moves around, disturbing the trim (and annoying the oarsman), but throughout this little voyage she sat remarkably still. However, as we approached the edge of the pond, when we were still a foot or so away from land, she made a sudden spring to terra firma.

We carried the coracle to the Plume of Feathers, a pub not far from the nearest park gate and closer than those on the riverside. The coracle had a strap fixed to the thwart so that it could be carried on a person's back, with the handle of the paddle stuck in another loop and the paddle over one's shoulder, taking some of the coracle's weight. We posed for more photographs by a plate marking the Meridian on the wall of a house backing onto the park, and then sat, a few yards east of zero degrees, in the forecourt of the Plume. We drank the pub's beer, rather than the bottle Piet had brought to the launching, to celebrate the arrival of the coracle and to welcome the Robsons. It was a lovely bright May evening, the partial eclipse having happened without me, at least, being fully aware of it. Margie Robson asked Margot: "Where did you get it?" And I asked: "And how did you get it here?"

Margot said that at a Christmas party she had met Neil Cossons, the new director of the Maritime Museum. He had come from the Ironbridge Gorge Museum on the Severn River in Shropshire, where he had directed the conservation of several early Industrial Revolution sites. Mr. Cossons had told her that there lived at Ironbridge a man, Eustace Rogers, who was probably the last coracle maker in England, if not the entire British Isles. The museum at Greenwich had one of his coracles on display.

Margot went to see this, decided a coracle was to be my birthday present, and wrote to order one from Mr. Rogers at his home, Severnside, Ironbridge, Shropshire. Delivery was promised for early May. When that time came, she told a completely unsuspecting me that she was going to visit Liz, then teaching in a school near Birmingham, and was taking along Liz's boyfriend, David Kelly, a postgraduate engineering student. What I wasn't told was that on the long way round to see Liz, Margot and David went to Ironbridge, twenty-five miles northwest of Birmingham, and collected the coracle. It stayed overnight at Liz's, going up and down nine floors in the elevator of the block of flats where she lived. Then it returned to London on top of the car and was quite at home for several weeks at the Maritime Museum, courtesy of Piet, until it was brought forth today.

At dinner, Margot produced some photographs she had taken at Ironbridge showing Mr. Rogers demonstrating the handling of the coracle on the Severn, just below his cottage, while in the background, arching across the river, was to be seen the first cast-iron bridge, built in 1779, from which the village takes its name. A fortnight later, Piet called in with photographs he had shot at the launching in the park. A large cast, and how pleased people looked! In many of the photographs, I for one was to be seen with a smile of pure happiness. It is, surely, rare to receive a birthday present that is an absolute surprise and delight and that promises surprises and delights to come.

From the window of my room in the Tontine Hotel, the graveled surface of the bridge seems to make a broad but personal path to the hillside across the river. March sun creating deep shadows within the gorge. Frost on the

bridge gravel lasts long in the mornings, since the bridge
has been closed to traffic for more than fifty years and
is trodden at this hour only by people who live in the
cottages on the far side and who walk across to shop in
Ironbridge or to wait at the bus stop for transport to take
them up to the new town of Telford. From my window,
I cannot actually see the river. It is running fifty feet
below the center of the cast-iron arch, which is—according to Eustace—mounted on piers one hundred feet and
six inches apart (the arch therefore forms a nearly
perfect semicircle, or circle when reflected in calm
water). Ironbridge is an extension of the much older
community of Coalbrookdale and is built mostly on the
steep northeastern slope of the gorge that the Severn has
furrowed here. Coalbrookdale was originally Caldebrook-
dale, meaning the valley of the cold stream—the brook a
tributary of the Severn—and it provided the British
birthplace of modern industry because the local hills
bear coal, iron ore, tar, and clay, and the rivers furnished
waterpower and water transport.

Eustace lives in "the Dip," the lowest level of the
village: half a dozen cottages on a narrow terrace of
land, fronted by a footpath about twenty feet above the
river, and a hundred yards or so downstream of the
bridge. I walk down after breakfast; the path and steps
descend behind the war memorial, the granite plinth
with names of the fallen surmounted by a statue of a
Shropshire infantryman in World War I uniform, the
clothes seeming too large for the frail figure within.
Halfway down, I can see whether a plume of gray smoke
is rising from Eustace's kitchen chimney or whether a
door is open in the long shed that forms his workshop or
whether he is out working in his garden. Eustace feels
free to talk after he has, in his words, "got going and

fed the animals." These are a one-eyed tortoiseshell cat referred to as "Little'un" or "Mate"; two ferrets, one brown, one blond, kept in cage-doored boxes at the edge of his vegetable patch; and a varying quantity of ducks, including several pair of mallards and a white domestic duck gone wild, which come up from the river for a daily handout. This is the smallest number of creatures the Rogers establishment has sustained for some years. Eustace's father, Harry, generally had half a dozen dogs, a score of ferrets, a tame fox or two, a badger, and a number of birds, including a jackdaw, to which he often talked. One of Harry Rogers's foxes, named Billy, used to take itself for long walks downriver, but always returned at night. To Harry Rogers, a wild fox was "Rennard" and a badger was "Brock." Eustace's dogs take the form of two pieces of privet hedge he has trimmed into terrier shape, one on each side of the path leading to the front door. Two other items of topiary are shrubs cut in a way that makes one think of the flared skirts of ballet dancers. A single red-and-white gnome sits to one side of the doorway, while the brass door knocker is an impression of a full-rigged man-of-war.

Eustace is seventy-one and lives alone in the house, a few yards from the site of the long-demolished cottage where his grandparents lived and maybe his great-grandparents. He was born on August 5, 1914, the day after the First World War was declared, in the house of his mother's family, a hundred and fifty yards up the hill. He has two sisters, both married, one of whom lives in a cottage a few doors away along the Dip, the other living in Broseley, a town two miles away across the river. The hillside of the gorge comes close to the back of the house, where a heavy-timbered table bears the skeleton of a coracle under construction, and a run-down conservatory, used for storing garden tools and firewood, shelters the approach to the back door. I tap on the side window, seeing Eustace within reading the *Daily Mirror*; he beckons me inside. The back door is just ajar, for Eustace is not worried by cold drafts—indeed, may welcome air in the back room (a sort of dining-living room), where an old-fashioned range with open iron fireplace and side oven sometimes smokes badly, because of downdrafts off the hillside. After trying different sorts of chimney pots to combat this phenomenon, Eustace has set up a deflector of sheet steel, propped over the fire on one log and one brick of equal height. The room has a smoky tinge to it, made more evident by a thin beam of March sunlight filtering through the one window. Eustace offers me "a drink of tea" from the brown teapot. It sits on a square table, which is covered by an old newspaper, on which also rests a small, elderly television set. Two wooden armchairs are on each side of the table, one a rocking chair, and motioning me toward this, facing the fire, Eustace resumes his seat in the chair which was his father's and his grandfather's. The faded houndstooth-check cap he is wearing is set slightly aslant, revealing straight gray hair. He is also wearing an open shirt with a kerchief knotted at the throat, two cardigans one over the other, a navy-blue donkey jacket with the faded letters CEGB (for "Central Electricity Generating Board") on the back, black work trousers, and heavy black boots. On a brass hook to the left of the fireplace is a cap that appears to be exactly the same as the cap he is wearing. From a brass rail under the mantelpiece hangs a pair of woolen socks.

Our talk is occasionally interrupted as Eustace goes to the conservatory for a log or a shovel of coal for the fire, or to one of the two front rooms for a book, a photograph, or some papers, found—in drawers or boxes or in piles under a piece of furniture—with no great difficulty, though he apologizes for the dusty, disordered conditions and what he calls "all this lumber." He adds, "It's what happens when you're on your own." Eustace has light gray eyes at once innocent and keen, and a Shropshire country way of talking—a hint of Welsh in the accent, and occasional usages like "me" instead of "my" (as in "me Dad") and "thee" instead of "thy," for "your." He talks of his family with a reverence and affection that doesn't preclude humor, particularly if a story concerns himself. Describing how he was born just uphill at his maternal grandparents', he says, "So I've always felt like a foreigner down here." It would be hard to imagine anyone more evidently at home.

Eustace was the name of one of his uncles. His friends and acquaintances in Ironbridge for the most part call him Eusty. His grandfather Tommy Rogers worked on the last river barges, built coracles, fished, eeled, and poached. Eustace's father, Harry Rogers, was a forager, rabbit catcher, coracle builder, and seasonal farm worker. Eustace went in a coracle for the first time when he was nine and had just learned to swim (his father would not sell a coracle to a nonswimmer), but before that he started accompanying his father on rabbiting expeditions. "I remember, oh, a very early memory, one night my father said, 'Come on,' and we walked in the dark to Buildwas, two mile, and we met a gamekeeper, Bill Witterick, waiting under a tree. He said to my father, 'What's brought the dog for, Harry?' Dad said, 'It's not the dog, it's the lad.' I was holding onto his coat so as not to get lost. The gamekeeper helped us put out the rabbit nets. You had to be in with the gamekeepers; we never interfered with their pheasants."

Eustace went to primary school in Ironbridge, where he was good at arithmetic. "Oh, I could top the class in that. When I was eleven, we were coming back from Madeley up on the hill one day from football, and Mr. Wragg, the headmaster, asked if I could sit for the scholarship to the grammar school. I asked my father, and he said no, 'You'd look good going to the grammar school with the seat worn out of your trousers.' I left school in 1928, before I was fourteen. The headmaster said he knew of a job for me, but I said, 'I'm going with my dad, rabbit catching.' "

Eustace reckons that his father, Harry, got three-quarters of his livelihood from or by way of the river. "We were reared on rabbits and fish." After 1926, the coracle could not be used legally for netting salmon, but it was handy for laying out eel lines, for salvaging driftwood, and for carrying home the catch on rabbiting expeditions. When the Severn was in flood, rabbits were often marooned on banks or in parts of fields that had become islands. A coracle was the perfect craft for a forager and his rabbit net on such occasions. It would be carried several miles upstream and, when the rabbits had been caught, loaded up and paddled back down-stream. In the days of Eustace's grandfather, rabbiting was often considered to be poaching, and the enemies were gamekeepers, landowners, the police, and magis-trates (who were generally local landowners). But in Harry Rogers's time the rabbit was regarded by farmers as a pest as well as food, and the rabbit catcher was recognized as a useful fellow; farmers would appoint a catcher for their land and, though never giving the rabbits away, would come to an arrangement for their taking—so much an acre, or the catch split fifty-fifty. Harry Rogers's dogs and ferrets were part of his rabbiting gear. The catching season was from harvest time to March, when the foragers wisely desisted, knowing that otherwise they would be robbing themselves of rabbits in following seasons. So, in spring and early summer, Harry Rogers hired himself out as a vermin hunter, worked in brickyards, and built a coracle or two.

Eustace says that the craft of rabbit catching involved knowing not only where the rabbits were but how to use the wind and the lie of the land. If you saw the clouds blowing from a certain direction, you knew one field was preferable to another. Rabbits might, for instance, come from a wood to a field to the south, and if the wind was in the south the catchers would place their nets between field and wood, then creep round back to the field to windward, so that the rabbits caught the scent of man. This drove the rabbits in a panic back toward the woods, and into the net. The rabbits were dispatched by hand, with a brisk twist of the neck, which Eustace demonstrates in the air. "Some days, my father got one hundred and fifty rabbits. We created a name for such clean rabbits, not shot or hurt by dogs, that people came for miles to buy them. Half a crown was the most we ever asked for one—that was during the war. I never got tired of eating rabbit. We would have rabbit for Christmas dinner, me and my dad, while the rest of the family was eating cockerel. I remember when myxomatosis first broke out, thirty-five years ago, and that seemed to put an end to it. Once after that, up near Buildwas, I caught a lovely rabbit, unmarked by the disease. I let it go. Three years ago, a farmer told me rabbits were back, eating his wheat. I went and caught three or four hundred. Then last year I went to the same farm again and found that the myxomatosis had returned—it keeps coming back, though some rabbits are immune—and they didn't need me."

Most of Eustace's life has been taken up with work more regular than that done by his father and grand-father. From the ages of fifteen to forty, he was a farm worker; for twelve years, he served as a cowman on a farm two miles from Ironbridge, cycling to and from work every day, and then some nights going foraging with his father. He used to arrive at the farm at 6:30 a.m. "We had thirty-five milkers, all done by hand, and the milk wagon came at 8 a.m. Sometimes on light nights I was there till 10 p.m. There was thatching, and hedge laying, and making stacks. Just about everything was done by hand—hay to be carried, mangels to be pulped. For twelve years, I never had a day off. I worked Sunday, Good Friday, Christmas Day. There was very little money in it, but I'm not complaining. If I had my time on earth again, I'd not change it." Eustace was paid twelve shillings and sixpence a week when he began. "I gave ten bob to my mother and kept half a crown for spending money." Farm wages were then the lowest manual wage in Britain, but the work was steady, and he got on well with his employer, Ryde Drury—"one of the rummest buggers in the world, but a good farmer and a good man." Eustace's mother ran a thrifty house-hold. "If she couldn't afford it, she didn't buy it. Frost and snow meant my father couldn't do much, and they sometimes lasted six weeks. We didn't have the welfare state."

At about the time myxomatosis was introduced and cut down rabbiting, Eustace gave up farming and went to work at Buildwas Power Station. This is a huge coal-fired electricity-generating plant dominating the water meadows alongside the Severn, at the northern approach to the Ironbridge gorge. There, one of his main jobs was at the intake bringing in river water for cooling purposes; with a large rake, he had to keep the grids clear of riverborne debris. "It was a rough job in winter, but it was out of doors and clean, away from the coal dust." He retired with a pension from the CEGB when he was sixty-two; the power station was enlarged, and four immense cooling towers reduced the need for Severn water. Since that time, Eustace has, among other things, been building more coracles per year than his father or grandfather ever did.

Living in one spot over several generations, the Rogerses acquired property. Eustace showed me an old deed, beautifully penned, for a piece of land, just across the river, that used to belong to his family. He is still vexed with his father for having given away the steep garden behind his present home when the owners of the inn above, the Three Tuns, expressed a desire for it. He is, however, proud of his father for his actions in the late 1930s, which made possible this house and the continuance of the way they lived. In the mid-nineteenth century, another pub, the Coopers' Arms, occupied part of the land here along the towpath. It lost its license in the 1870s and was turned into three dwellings, one of which became the Rogerses' leasehold home. In 1935, the local authority, the Wenlock District Council, declared the cottages unfit for habitation; two were already abandoned. The Rogerses were given notice to leave but did not. Eustace's father was irate. "The old man said, 'First man as sets foot in this house, he's dead.' He told me to fetch a shotgun from the farm and buy some cartridges. 'Don't be so bloody soft,' I told him, but I could see he meant it, and brought him a gun. He was defending his life." The case took two years to come to the Ironbridge Police Court; when it did, in 1937, it was an Ironbridge *cause célèbre*.

Eustace has photographs, from the time, of his father wearing a similar cap to his own, a spotted kerchief round his neck, moleskin waistcoat, corduroy trousers, boots, and gaiters; independence in the gaze, and in the smile a little mischief. To the magistrates of the court, he was described as a rabbit catcher, aged fifty. The clearance order made by the Council had been confirmed by the Ministry of Health. Notice to quit had been served on the defendant, who had not complied; a house in a Council estate at Hill Top, Madeley, was available for him. Mr. Lanyon, Harry Rogers's solicitor, pointed out to the court that his client earned his living from the river and kept a number of dogs and ferrets on his premises. Would he be permitted to keep them in the house offered? Mr. Fergusson, assistant town clerk of Much Wenlock, said, "He would not. He may be permitted to keep one dog." Mr. Lanyon said that the Rogers family had lived in this spot for over a hundred years. Mr. Rogers was a coracle maker. It was necessary for him to be by the river. There was a possible solution. The owner of the land on which the house stood was prepared to let Mr. Rogers buy the land for a nominal sum if Mr. Rogers provided suitable plans for a new house and the Council approved the plans.

Harry Rogers then gave evidence. He said it was necessary for him to have a number of dogs. "One dog is no use," he added, "for he is rheumatic, he is done for.

I have four dogs and that's not enough. If they gave me the house at Hill Top, it would be no use to me. If I went to Madeley, I would pick my pallbearers before I went."

Mr. G. L. Peace, for the Council, said, "You understand that if this suggestion is accepted, the Council cannot keep the house at Hill Top open for you."

Mr. Rogers: "I never asked them to build it. I don't want it."

Samuel Moseley of Cannock, joiner and builder, said in evidence that he was prepared to erect a cottage on this land for Harry Rogers, who was his brother-in-law.

The case was adjourned while the Council decided what to do. Finally, the Council agreed to allow Harry Rogers to build a new house in the Dip.

A good omen: a new wooden wheelbarrow came floating down the Severn and was plucked ashore by Harry Rogers in his coracle, just when they needed it. They salvaged bricks and timber from the demolished cottages. Much of the rest of the timber, including several fine oak beams, had come from the river. Samuel Moseley provided plans and expertise, Eustace helped his father dig the footings, and a bricklayer worked for them on weekends. The house took nine weeks to build; it was planted a little farther back from the river than the demolished cottages, and a little higher; it has never been flooded, unlike the other cottages that remain in the Dip. "The water's come to the gate," says Eustace, "but no higher."

Eustace now points out curiosities in the construction —how the bricks are slightly thicker at the front of the house, so that those at the back and sides required more mortar between each course. The mortar was a mix of three to one, sand to cement, stronger than necessary.

The house has heavy concrete lintels, painted white, over the windows, and the front door is smack in the middle, with a porch built around it; there is something ecclesiastical in shape about the porch and its glasswork. The front door knocker, Eustace tells me, is a representation of Nelson's flagship at Trafalgar, the *Victory*.

Eustace knows the river well for about twelve miles upstream and six down. He is sensitive to its moods. "Severn," he calls it, not "the Severn." It is the longest river in Britain, rising in the Welsh mountains upon Plynlimon, tumbling, then winding in big loops into the Welsh Marches, passing through such cathedral cities as Worcester and Gloucester, and debouching into the Bristol Channel's extreme tides. Ironbridge is about halfway from source to mouth. Eustace says the Severn here can rise or fall ten to twelve feet overnight, may change from a placid, slowly moving stream deep in the gorge one day to a massive body of water in spate the next. "If it was blowing a gale from the west, Dad would say, even if there wasn't a spot of rain here, 'Now get ready for Severn in the morning.' He knew it would be raining up in the mountains, feeding the headwaters. If the wind was southwest, he knew there'd be less to worry about—it would be the Teme, which enters the Severn at Worcester, well downstream of here, that would be rising." On Eustace's shed is posted an official riverboard notice: "WARNING! This river is extremely DANGEROUS and *not* suitable for bathing." A life ring is hung on a post near one of his topiary bushes. Eustace points out that floods can occur in different places at different times: 1946 saw the highest recorded in Ironbridge; 1947 the highest in Stourport, which is twenty-five miles downstream. Since then, dams and reservoirs have been built up in the mountains, and according to Eustace, the river's behavior has ceased to be so devastating. "There's been no great flood since then, though we're not sure there won't be another."

In the last hundred years, the riverbanks have changed a good deal. The former towpath, along which horses trudged as they pulled barges upstream, has in many places fallen in, been fenced across, or become overgrown. Banks have collapsed where there were once wharves and warehouses. Eustace's grandfather sometimes worked on the river barges, and went on one of their last voyages. "The final trip downstream my granddad made was with a load of fire bricks from here. My father used to say it was a very rough day. A chimney stack blew down at Coalbrookdale. When the barge reached Bridgnorth, the man at the tiller lost control. The barge got athwart the current, hit the bridge, and sank. Several years later, the barge was raised and towed up to Shrewsbury, but already shrubs and saplings were growing on the towpath. They had to be cut down, and hurdles moved aside that landowners had put across the path, to enable the horses to get through."

The river in this midsection is by no means a water-filled trench of uniform width and depth but is a succession of pools, irregularly interspersed with shallows, old fords, and former weirs (both natural and man-made), of stretches where it runs for a long period through flat ground, and then places—sometimes with rocks and other obstructions—where it falls sharply over a short distance. In the section of the river just downstream of here, between Ironbridge and Coalport, the Severn falls roughly eight feet in two miles. The riverside placards put up by the Ironbridge Museum Trust

refer to it as "Canoeists' White Water," while Eustace
calls it "the rapids, the worst stretch on the river—you
can stand with the water up to your knees in one place
and then it's forty feet deep the next." The river's often
placid appearance is beguiling, tempting people to swim
in it—though they do so less now than in the past.
Eustace remembers his father saying, after a spell of fine
weather suddenly broke, "Get ready, they'll be needing
us," and soon enough they were. Eustace's grandfather
rescued many people from the river; he recovered numerous bodies, including those of two gamekeepers, whose
punt had capsized, a year after they had drowned.
Harry Rogers had a similar record of lifesaving and re-
covery. In the "long flood" of March 1947, he took food
and coal by coracle to riverbank families marooned in
their upstairs rooms. "When there were tragedies on the
river, they always came to us to help," says Eustace. "We
never accepted a ha'penny for doing it." Eustace, to his
regret, has never saved a life, but has pulled out several
bodies. One was that of a four-year-old boy, three years
ago; another was that of an elderly lady, whom a doctor
tried to resuscitate, but who did not survive. Eustace
prefers to talk about the happier finds the Rogers family
have been well situated to make. On one occasion, a dog
came downriver, standing on the roof of its kennel, to
which it was chained, barking loudly, and was rescued by
Eustace and his father. Harry Rogers regarded anything
floating downriver as rightly his, and anglers sitting on
the far bank would often alert him with the cry "Flotsam!" He would then appear from the shed, launch his
coracle, and waylay, for example, the limb of a tree; he
would hammer in a nail or staple, attach a line, and
tow it to the bank. Apart from the wheelbarrow, he

rescued a fruit cart and a small truck, which took more than the gear at the Rogerses' disposal to haul out. Eustace says there are fewer such trophies in the river now.

The shed has been there for fifty-three years. It is roughly thirty feet long, ten feet wide, with its wooden walls painted red on the outside, and a corrugated-steel roof. It stands on the river side of the footpath, with the grassy bank falling away steeply beneath it to the Severn. Eustace works in the shed daily in three out of four seasons. "I've been foolish enough now and then to go buggering around in there in winter, but you're the loser when you do. It's often colder in than out, and then you can get laid up from it." Eustace's is the shed of sheds, the apotheosis of the tarred and creosoted wooden huts that stand in many a British garden and allotment, forming workshop and storage place, refuge and re-pository for stuff that may come in useful one day. It contains, of course, a workbench—twelve feet long—and tools for woodworking, some up-to-date with painted and varnished handles, many with the dusty, rusty, and pitted brown-black of age. Objects line the walls, lie on shelves and benches, rest on the rafters, or stand on the floor to be squeezed past. The shed contains five coracles: up in the rafters are one of Eustace's calico-covered type and a Shrewsbury model, almost rectangular; the three standing on edge on the floor, all built by Eustace, con-sist of one cowhide version and two new calico-covered, one finished, one still awaiting its coat of bitumen. I note coils of rope and line, a disconnected stove, lengths of chain, nets, fishing tackle, a miner's lamp, walking sticks, stacks of timber, heaps of wood shavings, jars of nails and screws, a chimney cleaning brush, and a six-foot-six-inch-long, two-man timber-felling saw with shark-like teeth. Eustace's one-eyed cat is asleep in the cobweb-filled shed window that faces the river and is warmed by the sun. As we edge along, Eustace tells me the name or nature of tools and devices I don't recognize. There is a scoop for pouring molten metal. There are some implements for sampling cheese. There are tailor's shears, sixteen inches long and four pounds in weight. There is a barbed device for dragging along the riverbed to recover eel lines. There are traps for catching moles, badgers, foxes, and birds. There is a device for crimping the ends of refilled shotgun cartridges. There is a "barnacle," a claw-shaped double hook for putting in a bull's nostrils. There is a thirty-year-old but seemingly unused wheelbarrow, with massive timbers and an iron-shod wheel, which Eustace made as a copy of the barrow that came from the river, before it wore out. There is a gas mask from the First World War with a hose like an elephant's trunk leading to a filter. There are several pairs of old clamp-on ice skates; two lawnmowers; many kinds of spade; leather kneecaps; gum boots; punt poles; a faded nineteenth-century photograph of a threshing team; and a number of chains, with china handles, for working the overhead cisterns of toilets. There is a trunk full of fishnets and a box of wooden net-knitting needles. Eustace says, "In wintertime we'd sit making nets, my dad on one side of the fireplace, me and one of my sisters on the other. It was a lovely pastime. But we were finished with fishnets in the late twenties, when they made netting illegal. After that, we made rabbit nets, pig nets, even nets for football goalposts."

Various people who visit Eustace's shed covet certain items. An Australian took a fancy to the china chain pulls. One local man, Reg Morton, who helped set up the

Ironbridge Museum, hoped that most of it might go to form a Rogers Room in the museum whenever Eustace died or retired—a proposition that Eustace didn't know how to answer, though Mr. Morton died before it was in any way pressed. Children who come into the shed are generally fascinated by a number of large movable figures, made by a former coal miner called Jack Gears who was a friend of Eustace's, and designed to cross the Severn on a wire which Harry Rogers rigged across the river. This was all in aid of a celebration of the bicentenary of Coalbrookdale in 1959. One figure is that of a witch on a broomstick; another, that of a man pedaling on a single wheel. "Jack Gears never had a home of his own," says Eustace. "He was always in lodgings. He made one of his friends a set of false teeth and another an artificial arm, though he couldn't work out a handgrip. A Birmingham firm that made artificial limbs wanted him to go to work for them, but he wouldn't leave here. Aye, he was clever, Jack was. Only it wasn't used, except in a small way."

One small lidless box in the shed contains various items that Eustace for some reason has collected here rather than in the house: photographs, postcards, newspaper clippings, two books, and a scholarly article about coracles from a 1936 issue of *The Mariner's Mirror*. Most of the postcards are of local views, but two were sent to him from London; the scenes are Piccadilly Circus and Buckingham Palace. Eustace has never been to London, though he has been to Birmingham, to Rhyl in North Wales, and, the farthest, to Southport, a seaside resort seventy miles away in Lancashire, on a day trip by coach. One photograph, roughly a century old, shows several people, among them a lady in a long white dress, posed curiously far apart outside the Tontine Hotel.

Another of similar vintage portrays the Ironbridge Division of the Shropshire Constabulary—ten fearsome big men in blue. The two books are even older, both with injured spines and battered boards. One is the first volume of *Belisarius*, a novel by Madame de Genlis, published in translation by Henry Colburn in London in 1808. The other is the fifth volume of *Tristram Shandy*, MDCCLXII; i.e., the first edition.

I pick it up with care. The front board is coming away. Eustace says, "The books belonged to Nacky, a fisherman who lived for a while with my grandparents. Nacky used to keep his feathers, for making flies, pressed inside them." I turn the pages. Tristram, and Corporal Trim, and Uncle Toby! Eustace senses my interest. It is difficult not to emulate the Australian chain-pull fancier and Mr. Morton. Eustace says, "I've read a little bit of it. It's one of the early ones—amazing how it's lasted. It don't make much sense to me, but I expect you should make an allowance—they didn't know much better then." Nacky was one of Grandfather Rogers's fishing and poaching companions, and although his real name, according to Eustace, was Jim Hill, he went by the name of Nacky Brady. In the *Shandy* volume, someone—I presume, Nacky—had written in sepia ink several lists of local place-names, perhaps denoting spots where fish were to be found. In the back is an untutored drawing of a man on a beast, with the caption "Thomas Brading on his donkey." So perhaps Brading or Brady was his real name and Jim Hill was a mysterious pseudonym.

It is cold, standing in the shed, and we move back to the house, to one of the front downstairs rooms, where Eustace lights the gas fire and finds a stack of old scrapbooks. He is still thinking about Nacky. He says, "Nacky didn't do a regular day's work in his life; he just fished and poached. He was born with a caul covering his face. That meant he was all right on the river—he'd never get drowned. He was only a slight man, no weight hardly. One night—he had turned seventy then—he landed here with a coracle full of rabbits. There was a policeman waiting for him, and in the tussle Nacky was tipped in. He swam back over to the other side, climbed out, walked up to Buildwas and across the bridge and back here. He found his coracle next morning two and a half miles downriver, upside down, with the bag of rabbits still underneath, held by the vacuum."

The river men of Eustace's grandfather's day have a Homeric status in and around Ironbridge, worthy of rank alongside other Shropshire heroes such as Old Parr, who was said to have been 152 years old when he died in 1635, and Captain Matthew Webb, who was born in Ironbridge and lived in nearby Dawley, the first man to swim the English Channel (in 1875). Tommy Rogers, Eustace's grandfather, was born in 1843 and died in 1925 and often swam with Captain Webb, before the latter died trying to swim the rapids under Niagara Falls. Tommy Rogers was a large man who weighed nearly 280 pounds. "He was one of the toughest, hardest-drinking buggers in the world," says Eustace. Well into middle life, he boxed annually at the Ironbridge Fair, and in 1923, when he was seventy-nine, he took part in the diving contest at the Ironbridge Regatta. He disappeared after a dive and many thought he had drowned, but he was discovered hiding behind a bush across the river, laughing at those searching for him. Tommy had two sons, Harry and Jim, and two daughters, both of whom emigrated to Canada. In 1862, Tommy Rogers, aged eighteen, was the first person to be tried for poaching at the court in the new Ironbridge police station, and was given a three-months sentence. "There were fifteen poachers along here," says Eustace, "and maybe half of them in jail at any one time. They'd go out in the afternoon with nets under their jackets, over their shoulders or wrapped round their chests. They kept coracles along the river, where they might come in handy, or else they'd take one with them, for loading the rabbits into, then the others could walk home not worrying if they ran into a policeman." The police, according to Eustace, had nothing else to do in those days except chase poachers, and were spurred on by local landowners like "old man Kynnersley" at Leighton; there were duels between police and poachers, pitched battles, and assassinations. "The police drowned old John Goodwin," Eustace says, "but it was never proved—they got away with it."

Just before his death, Tommy Rogers realized that his sons would have difficulty getting his ample coffin down the steep and narrow stairs of the old cottage in the Dip if he died in his bedroom, so he told Harry and Jim to put him in the chair by the fireplace downstairs. Then he asked them to fetch a pint of best bitter from the Three Tuns. Ironbridge legend has it that he took a long draught of the beer, said "Goodbye, my bonny lads. I'm off among the straight-faced ones," placed his hands over his stomach, and without further ado crossed the great divide. According to Eustace, his Uncle Jim was nervous of what the neighbors would say if they saw that the proprieties of dying had been ignored, so he and Harry carried their father upstairs. Whence, in a coffin next day, they indeed found it hard to get him downstairs again.

Eustace's father never wore a watch. Eustace says,

"Time didn't bother him. Sundays were like any other day. He knew the Bible, though I never saw him reading it, and he only went to church for a funeral. He didn't drink like my granddad, and as long as he had tuppence for a packet of Woodbines he was happy. He had a hell of a sense of humor, and he could romance to an extreme. He kept saying he was going to take a coracle across the Channel, but he never did." Harry Rogers, one suspects, enjoyed giving anyone listening to one of his stories a good measure. In a BBC radio interview broadcast in October 1941, he said: "My chief manipulation of the coracle is eeling for eels, and this is how I make this pay. Five hundred hooks baited should be a profitable night, say about sixty pound of eels, shilling per pound, quick sale, most important thing is to know the haunts of the smaller bait, stone roach, better known as bull knobs, and Jack Sharpes, and camper eels, four inch long, they're all fixed into hook in a craftsmanship manner, laid in lines across the river from out of the coracle, and with cat stones attached to keep them on the bottom from night to daybreak, me on the riverbank camping in front of a good fire, with the old drumming-up tin always on the boil, and the silent of night in the air, and with my mind full of memories I long to think sweet of."

Harry Rogers often used to walk upstream along the now dismantled railway line, on the other side of the river, to Cressage, carrying his coracle. In one story Eustace likes retelling, Harry made such an excursion late in the afternoon of December 31, 1924. "The wind was howling out of the west," says Eustace, "and he was having a job to walk. He'd got to a row of twelve poplar trees we called the Apostles, and he was sitting having a rest when he saw another coracle coming along. It was old Nacky. Dad said it was such a wild night he didn't think it was worth going on. Nacky said, 'Oh, you're bloody frightened.' So they went on up the railway line, walking on the sleepers. It had got dark, but the moon was up. They were opposite Leighton, passing under an arch, when something told my father to get off the track. There was the wind, of course, and you can't hear a thing behind you when you're carrying a coracle. Dad used to say, 'I jumped aside and the next bloody moment there was the light of the engine. I thought as the train went by, Nacky's on the front of that engine and they'll be taking him off at Cressage Station. So, sadly, I set off home. I hadn't gone more than a few yards when there was a shout from up the bank. It was Nacky, still with his coracle. The wind had blown them there.' The gale continued, and Nacky and my dad took shelter in a platelayers' cabin. Nacky had a watch, which he consulted, and at midnight they wished each other a Happy New Year. Next day, they came down the river at dark with their coracles full of rabbits."

Eustace let me borrow from the shed box the article on coracles, and I took it up to the Tontine to read that evening. It was part of a scholarly two-part study that James Hornell, a noted small-craft historian, published in *The Mariner's Mirror* in 1936. Hornell may have sent it to Eustace's father, for there is among the illustrations a photograph of Harry Rogers, captioned "An Ironbridge Rabbit Catcher in His Coracle." From Hornell's work I learned that the British coracle, though related to the Irish seagoing curragh, is in fact a far older form, derived from the same common source as the bitumen-coated *guffa* of Iraq and the skin-covered coracles of India and Tibet. (Elsewhere, I read later that the Babylonians had coracles on the Euphrates, and that Herodotus had de-

scribed them as being "round as a shield.") Julius
Caesar provided the first record that we have of the craft
in Britain. Recounting his military experiences in Spain
c. 49 B.C., at a time when his communications had been
cut because of floods and the destruction of bridges,
Caesar said that he had ordered his men to make wicker-
work boats, covered with hides, of the kind that he had
learned about in Britain a few years before. Later Roman
writers referred to British skin-covered craft, whose use
was noticed in remote localities when iron tools were
generally making possible the construction of planked
boats. In the early Middle Ages, various Welsh writings,
in prose and poetry, mention coracles, usually as covered
with black bullock hides. Froissart, in his chronicles of
1360, describes the matériel used by Edward III's army
for the invasion of France, including six thousand carts
used for carrying tents and other equipment. "Upon
these carts were also carried many vessels and small boats
made very artfully of boiled leather." What preserved
the coracle for the next six hundred years was its suit-
ability for catching salmon in the shallow, rock-strewn
rivers of Wales and the border country between Wales
and England.

Very few changes in coracle construction seem to have
happened in the course of two millennia. One change
was the use of sawn laths instead of split ash or willow
branches in the making of the lattice framework, and
laths replacing plaited hazel or willow withies in the
making of the gunwale. Another was the substitution of
different materials in place of the hide covering: first,
flannel, introduced at the beginning of the seventeenth
century, and still in use in southwest Wales till about
1870; and then canvas or calico, which began to be used
from the end of the eighteenth century. These new

coverings needed to be coated with pitch and tar, but the resulting coracle was half the weight of a hide-covered craft. The size of a coracle remained the same as it had been when determined by the size of a single hide, and even in the 1930s the tarred calico covering was referred to as the skin or hide. And the basic design continued to be that of "a broad, ovate, latticed framework in the form of a shallow, wide-mouthed basket."

When Hornell wrote, the coracle was confined to some of the rivers of Wales and the Marches: the Teifi, the Towy, the Taf, the Cleddau, the Severn, and the Dee. On other rivers, like the Usk, the Wye, and the Monnow, coracles had disappeared, said Hornell, "within the memory of middle-aged residents . . . On the Scottish mainland, the last survivors danced on the turbulent bosom of the Spey, but that is a memory of many years ago." The practice of net fishing from coracles lasted in southwest Wales after it was banned elsewhere. Coracles were also used for retrieving ducks that had been shot and for crossing rivers where there were few bridges. Farmers used them to reach marooned animals and when washing sheep. For general angling purposes, they were immensely handy. Hornell writes: "Great are the advantages for angling in a rocky, shallow river of a coracle over any other kind of craft. A coracle draws so little water . . . that it can go almost anywhere; the paddler, using one hand only, can turn and twist it at will and shoot rapids and thread narrow channels in a way quite impossible in a canoe. When need be he may slip behind a boulder or a jutting rock, or hold on with a paddle, gaff or foot and so fish places out of reach of the angler in waders or in any other craft but a coracle. In his basket boat the angler can snuggle in safety against a rocky ledge in a back eddy with foaming white water on one side or perhaps on both." Coracle fishermen usually carried a wooden club or "knocker" for stunning any salmon they caught, for, as Hornell noted, "a lusty salmon is a dangerous guest in a flimsy coracle."

Hornell also noted that coracles had an indefinite life. The skins could be patched. New coverings could replace old. If a hole appeared, it could be blocked for the moment with the coracle man's cap, his foot pressed down on it, while he paddled for the bank as if the devil were after him. Most coracle owners carried in their pockets an old piece of pitched calico, which they could warm at the edges with a match and plaster over the hole. Coracles, when finally worn out, were burned; the tar ensured that they made a fine bonfire. Hornell thought this practice might be a relic of an ancient rite in which decrepit coracles were sacrificed to river gods. One Carmarthen man saved three old coracles to the end of the First World War and burned them, in celebration, on Armistice night.

At the time Hornell was writing, coracles still flourished on the Severn between Shrewsbury and Arley, a distance of some thirty-five miles. This was a shrinkage from 1914, when they had been found over a range of sixty miles from Welshpool to Bewdley. (Welshpool is in Monmouthshire, where coracles were often called thorrockles or truckles.) Severn coracles were specifically remarked upon by Camden in 1586 in his *Britannia*. When the early-nineteenth-century writer Samuel Ireland, author of *Views on the Severn*, tried to get a boat near Welshpool to take him down to Shrewsbury, he was offered a coracle, which he declined. (Eustace has a similarly named book, *Picturesque Views of the Severn*, by a writer named Harral, from about the same time, in which is mentioned the claim that a Severn man

once went in a coracle downriver and down the Bristol
Channel to Lundy Island, in the open waters of the
Atlantic; he spent a fortnight on the voyage, in fine
weather, "and returned to as many congratulations as
though he had performed the circumnavigation of the
globe." I have a book, *Walks and Talks of an American
Farmer in England*, by Frederick Law Olmsted, describing his journey on foot in 1850 south through
England from Liverpool with two companions. In
Shrewsbury, the future celebrated landscape architect,
then twenty-eight, saw "a number of anglers with *cur-
ricles* . . . a light portable boat . . . easily carried on one
arm.") According to Hornell, two Shrewsbury men
once took their coracles by rail to Buttington near
Welshpool and made a leisurely four-day return journey
downstream, fishing by day and camping by night.
Hornell said that the railways "class coracles as bicycles
in their tariff, presumably because they are one-man
vehicles." One Shrewsbury man, D. Craddock, had only
one leg (his left) but carried his own coracle, walking
with a crutch under his right armpit. In the 1930s, the
men of the Frankwell district of Shrewsbury often
walked northward out of town on Sundays and holidays,
carrying their coracles as far as Shelton Rough, a distance
of four miles. "Here they launch their coracles and spend
the rest of the day in restful pursuit of the Gentle Art,
the while they drift in easy stages down the river."

At Ironbridge, Hornell wrote, "the Severn brawls
through a deep gorge, magnificently picturesque but
wearisome to cross on foot, for the old iron bridge . . .
spans the river at a high level; besides this inconvenience,
a penny toll is levied on every foot passenger. So the
people in the depths of the gorge [i.e., about fifty
feet down] keep coracles handy, if only to cross to the

other side." In 1936, Hornell observed eight coracles in use in Ironbridge, with others south to Arley, most made by the Rogers brothers, Harry and Jim. "Formerly nearly every cottager had his own coracle, hung in a tree when not in use." The design of the Ironbridge coracle had stabilized in the form of a shallow bowl, the two ends equally rounded for ordinary use, though in coracles built for racing the fore-end was sharper and the length was increased. The only exception to the double-ended symmetry of the ordinary coracle was the position of the seat, placed slightly aft of amidships. The last coracle race at Ironbridge was in the mid-1920s. The racing coracles had names painted across their bottoms, visible therefore only when upside down. Some of the names in use on coracles in a race at Llandrinis Bridge, between Welshpool and Shrewsbury, on May 28, 1798, for a silver cup valued at five guineas, were *Nancy the Rower*, *Peggy*, and *Lucy*.

The claim is sometimes made on Eustace's behalf that he is the last coracle maker in England. To this, as he stands by the coracle construction table in the garden, he makes a modest objection: "That's never been my statement. I don't know what other men are doing. I think there's a man up in Shrewsbury who can make them still. He came down to get some waterproofing from me a few years back. Shrewsbury football team have a ground near Severn, and when the ball goes in the river they need a craft to get it out. They had an ordinary boat, but this man said a coracle would be better for the job." However, Eustace is most probably the only man who builds coracles regularly, and almost certainly the only one who can still construct the ancient hide-covered type. "How I came to do that was about fifteen year ago," he says. "There's one up in Elgin Museum in Scotland, from the River Spey, they think it's two hundred and fifty year old. The museum wanted a replica and asked me. I was able to get the materials and put it together. I now rear about four of the skin ones every year."

Eustace thinks that coracles may originally have been built upside down, with the ends of the bent splints or ribs stuck in the earth to hold the shape while the interweaving was going on. But he builds or rears his right way up ("rears" being a verb also used in the coopering trade, a barrel being reared rather than simply made). For the hide-covered coracle, the splints are of hazel, which Eustace soaks in hot water to make additionally pliable. At a point that will form the middle of the bottom, the splints are held temporarily in place by two wooden clamps bolted to the construction table. Lengths of string keep the ends of the splints, for the time being, at the desired width of the coracle, until the plaited willow or hazel withies forming the oval gunwale have been fastened in place. Willow is also woven in basketwork fashion at the bottom to form a floor, and then the work is left for a day or so to dry. When the seat has been fixed athwartships, the construction becomes less fragile, can be unfastened from the table, and turned over to receive the skin. "Then I'm away to the abattoir," says Eustace, "to ask for a good big hide. I soak it in alum and saltpeter for a week, in the tin bath. Then I stretch it over the coracle framework, tie it to the gunwale, and let it shrink in place." The rope used for tying the coracle to a riverbank stake is made from the hair of horses' tails, twisted together. Hides now cost thirty pounds or so each, and a rope requires eight or nine tails at a pound apiece. So the hide coracles are much more costly to make than the calico version—which Eustace builds on the same rig, six or so a year, varying each one slightly to suit the size and weight of the purchaser. (Eustace's 1984 price for a calico coracle was £70; his father charged two pounds ten shillings for one in 1935; the increase is less than that which has occurred in average British wages, or in the price of such other things as a basic car.)

Eustace is helped occasionally by a friend, Philip Barber, who is in his forties and has a regular job in a foundry. Eustace hopes that Philip may one day take over the coracle business from the last of the coracle-building Rogerses. "Without Philip I'd be struggling," he says. "He has a vehicle, so he's able to take me to the abattoir. He goes to the timber yard to look for ash for the laths and for the looms of the paddles. I've shown him all I can."

Eustace has a wider market for his coracles than any other coracle maker before him. Visitors come to Iron-bridge from all over the world and are intrigued by what they see there. The commander of the first British nuclear submarine, *H.M.S. Dreadnought*, bought two of Eustace's coracles, and a U.S. nuclear sub commander, Eli Hutchinson, bought one, which Eustace thinks may have traveled to the New World well underwater. A retired British Army general has one. Eustace's coracles have gone to Israel, Norway, and Australia. (In the winters, he keeps busy making model coracles, a foot in diameter, and two of these have gone to the Soviet Union with returning Russian tourists.) Trader Vic's restaurant in San Francisco bought two hide and twelve calico coracles a few years ago, and though Eustace appreciated the massive order, he has had doubts.

was upstream and Bridgnorth down. Both the amount of river traffic and the high sides of the gorge favored the building of a single-span bridge. In 1709, Abraham Darby had perfected the technique of smelting iron ore with coke, and since then cast iron had been made in the area, a relatively cheap, strong material for fireplaces and tools. In the 1770s, a Shrewsbury architect, Thomas Pritchard, made designs for a cast-iron bridge which excited the interest of the prominent ironmasters John Wilkinson and Abraham Darby III—it was the latter who, apparently amending Pritchard's design, undertook its construction. This was cautious, following traditional carpentry practice in some respects, with base plates held by dovetail joints and uprights secured to the five main ribs by wedges; a greater amount of iron was used than was subsequently found to be needed in bridges of such dimensions. But this was the first. It survived the great flood of February 1795, which severely damaged every other bridge on the Severn. Thereafter, iron bridges were in fashion—and the original figured in the itinerary of visitors to Shropshire. The bridge was featured in many of the pictures that artists of the Romantic Age painted and drew of the gorge, the fires from the blast furnaces luridly illuminating the shaggy slopes above the Severn. However, the demands of twentieth-century traffic proved too much for the first iron bridge. In 1909, a concrete bridge was built half a mile downstream and, being free while the iron bridge continued to demand tolls, attracted much of the traffic. In 1931, the iron bridge was closed to all vehicles; pedestrians could still walk across for a penny. In 1950, it was finally freed from toll. Much repair and restoration work was done in the early 1970s, and a concrete inverted arch constructed on the riverbed to prevent the bridge abutments from slowly sinking and moving toward one another. Eustace says, "This has stopped the abutments sliding together at about a tenth of an inch per year, but it may put the old ironwork under pressure." There are, he thinks, about sixty cracks in the iron sections; he examines them closely in his daily consideration of the landmark which is his close neighbor. He says, "I suppose it's only natural, when you've grown up with a thing so close, that it's a part of you. It hurts to see it damaged in any way. You feel protective about it. I was going to fetch my papers one evening a year or so ago. I met an American making a sketch of it. I said, 'What do you think to our bridge?' And he said, 'I'll tell you what I think. I think that, when they built this bridge, it was as great a feat as our men going to the moon.' "

Eustace's Uncle Jim worked in the Coalbrookdale Iron Works most of his life but retired for a while to Canada, where his sisters lived. He came back to Ironbridge to die, and his ashes were, as he wanted, scattered on the Severn from the bridge.

Ironbridge is one of half a dozen communities that have been incorporated in the new town of Telford. The center of Telford has been laid out for the automobile age, with covered shopping malls, vast car parks, and a network of new roads leading to modern housing estates and the older villages. Ironbridge itself has become one of the sought-after places to live in the district, with its artisan houses and laborers' cottages being fixed up as homes for computer engineers and affluent retired folk. After its Industrial Revolution heyday, the place had a long decline, but it now manifests a renewed and not completely satisfactory prosperity, of the kind that can overwhelm a spot which is pretty and quaint and has associations with real work mostly in the past. Hence, tourist buses, school parties, craft shops, antique dealers; high heels *and* farm boots; and still industrial smoke from the iron-casting works, and coal trucks rumbling down through Coalbrookdale to Buildwas Power Station.

Eustace is ambivalent about some of the changes that have occurred during his lifetime. Because Ironbridge no longer has an ironmonger's shop (it once had two), he takes a bus to Telford town center to buy nails and paint. Telford new town does not appeal to him. "They've brought the worst buggers in the country here," he says. "It's terrible for vandalism—you leave a car in one of those car parks overnight and they'll have the wheels off." He blames young yobbos from Telford for the theft of one of his ferrets a year ago. But he recognizes the need to revitalize the district, and Ironbridge in partic-ular. "It was an ideal spot, this, for the birth of industry. They'd got everything they needed, the right minerals, and little brooks racing down to drive their bellows and water hammers. When I was going to school, there were brick- and tileworks, china factories, foundries for rain-water pipes and gutters and fire grates. Then in the years between the wars, housing construction slowed down and many of those things weren't needed so much. The Coalport chinaworks moved to Stoke, where they'd been getting their clay. The working population moved out of Ironbridge, up to Madeley and Telford, and the heart went out of this place. Shops were empty. Here, in the Dip, there used to be sixty living. Now there's twelve."

The Ironbridge Trust was set up in 1965 and opened its first museum site four years later; the original Abraham Darby blast furnace was put on view. Now the old furnaces, warehouses, china kilns, steam engines, and canal machinery form a dispersed museum for the early Industrial Age, attracting a quarter of a million paying visitors a year and probably as many again who don't enter the exhibits but wander outside and enjoy the gorge scenery, eat and drink in the local pubs and cafés, and buy postcards and souvenirs, among which are ashtrays—floridly colored—with a central picture of Eustace in a coracle. Ironbridge does well out of the trade but grumbles about the invasion. Local feeling about some of the improvements taking place was nicely put a few years ago in a letter to the *Shropshire Star* by a lady named Mary Bloomfield, from the nearby village of Eaton Constantine:

This area was once inhabited by others like Jim Rogers, people who loved it in its wild and natural state. The dilapidation of its buildings was hidden by vigorous, verdant loveliness. Who cared about the state of the buildings when they could feast their eyes on Benthall Edge, the Rotunda, and the Severn flowing as from time immemorial between them?

When Mr. Neil Cossons and others involved in the museum at "Blesses Hill" wonder why the "locals" are lacking in enthusiasm for their efforts, perhaps this is one reason. It is no longer home, and its children have gone elsewhere to live, because there is no point in staying. So few are the familiar faces in the streets and shops, we are now the strangers.

Eustace sympathizes with this point of view but also partially disagrees with it. "To my way of thinking, the museum rescued this place. It's not exactly how we'd like it to be, I know, and it's not the way things were, but I've said to many: What stage would it have reached without the museum? It would have gone right to the bottom." Ironbridge may not be perfect, but Eustace quotes his father, who used to say, "I haven't seen anywhere I'd swop for this."

At seventy-one, Eustace is no longer an early riser, especially in winter. But he has his morning chores to fulfill. He gets his own breakfast and a bite to eat at lunchtime, and goes daily to his sister in the Dip for his "tea"—his evening meal. Shopping in Ironbridge, he calls at Tim Eley's butcher shop, where the pork pies are still made on the premises, and goes to the post office for a money order to include with his weekly entry for the football pools. In the late afternoon, going to get his evening paper, he calls in on the lady at the antique shop to see if she wants one, too. He reads the *Daily Mirror*—a tabloid which has traditionally supported the Labour Party—in the morning, and the *Shropshire Star*, published in Shrewsbury, in the evening. He generally completes the *Mirror*'s crossword and cryptic puzzles, and sometimes clips items from its Codgers' column, which prints queries and replies about old gadgets and customs, such as the date when mantraps, for catching poachers, were made illegal—the answer being 1827, though they were still occasionally used after that. He has lived alone since the death of his mother in 1967, but he isn't lonely. If reference is made to the fact that he has never married, he repeats the adage, "Anyone who knew me wouldn't have me," or, still hiding slightly within the camouflage of quotation, "My dad used to say, 'Stay single and bring thee kids up the same.' " Old friends often drop in, sometimes bringing cakes made by their wives, and sit chatting by the fire with a pot of tea. They talk about the good fields for rabbits, and the time the ice was five inches thick on the Severn outside the power-station inlets, and the wars between poachers and land-lords. Eustace reads aloud from his books and documents. He reads slowly but precisely, having no difficulty with obscure words or complicated constructions. He says that he didn't put pen to paper from the time he left school until the war, when a friend went into the army and Eustace wrote to him. He himself as a skilled farm worker wasn't called up, but he volunteered for the Home Guard. "I wasn't very regular in attending," he says. "I had this letter telling me to report and I went along, bloody terrified. The captain told me they had decided to put me in the Intelligence section. Then he asked why I hadn't turned up recently. I said, the harvest. He said, then get back to it and get the harvest in. That was my last Home Guard appearance."

Although Eustace denounces hooligans and vandals, he thinks some of them may have been driven to unsocial behavior by their blank lives; he is not at all sympathetic to Mrs. Thatcher's government, which strikes him as not caring for the needs of many British people. "I've worked for this lot who are in power now. I had no choice but to work. And I know, they want you *down there*. Take Mr. Drury, the farmer I worked for—I admired him, and he admired me, but he didn't want me to change my station in life. Well, it pleases me when a working man can buy his own house and have a seaside holiday. I never wanted a car, though I could have had one, but I've wanted it for others. It upsets me that there's bloody millionaires thinking about how to make another mil-lion and not much about the people whose work goes into making it."

Eustace's view of society is by no means short, or un-documented. He finds in the front-room archives a sealed and witnessed parchment, the last will of William

Goodwin, 1778, which somehow came into the possession of the Rogers family. He reads out from the copperplate script various bequests of several hundred pounds each to relatives and retainers, the equivalent of many thousands today. Mr. Goodwin had all that, is Eustace's implication, while workmen in field and factory were living in hovels on crusts. "There have been some improvements, I know. A man out of work today is in some ways better off than a working man in the 1930s. Then you could be living from day to day even if you had a job. A man I knew at the Dale works said to me, 'We were paid on Friday, we were ready for payday again by Sunday.' I've worked alongside men who had wives and children and lived in tied cottages, owned by the farmers, and were terrified of losing their jobs, which meant losing their homes. What I've noticed is, when the working man's doing well, the country is doing well. The workman who is decently off wants to improve his home—he spends his money on carpets and paints. It keeps things going. The spending makes work. But this lot don't seem to understand. I don't know where we'd have been without that North Sea oil. You'd have been able to count our ribs, without that oil."

Eustace is not complaining about his own life, which seems to him to have been unbeatable, full of hard work and essentially independent. "I say I haven't been anywhere on holiday, and my mates reply, 'Your life has been one long bloody holiday.' It's been a life of experiences. I've never had a moment when I couldn't occupy myself by going out in a coracle, on a bike, or on foot." On Saturday afternoons, he sometimes walks to farms where he and his father used to go rabbiting, and admires the woods and fields. "When you've grown up as a countryman, you look at a tree and think 'That's a fine oak,' or 'What a lovely beech.' You glance at a field and say to yourself, 'That's a nice crop of swedes.' You know the name of what you're looking at—though don't think for a moment you know everything about it. If you thought that, you'd be fooling yourself." On these jaunts, Eustace keeps an eye open for willow and ash, useful for coracle making and for walking sticks, which —along with the model coracles—he fashions during the winter months. Occasionally, he will assist in "brushing" a hedge. He recently helped a friend cut back an overgrown hawthorn hedge which hadn't been dealt with in fifty years, and got out of the job two winters' supply of firewood. He works hard on his own garden, mowing and rolling the lawns, trimming the topiary and hedges, digging in the vegetable patch, where the cabbages, which should have been ready to pick by now, have been held up by late winter weather. His friends say he doesn't seem to have aged in the last fifteen years, though he is less shy: when he saw strangers approaching the shed, he would sometimes retreat to the house. He would still rather talk about his grandfather and father than about himself, but he is forthcoming about coracles, especially to frequent parties of schoolchildren. After school visits, he receives sheaves of illustrated thank-you letters and folders of drawings, perhaps with a crayoned title: "A Special Book for Mr. Rogers." The drawings generally feature the iron bridge and Eustace in a coracle. He may have learned that reticence—if not to draw attention to itself—involves being able to let yourself go a bit.

On weekday evenings, he watches sports on television or reads "gunslingers," paperback Westerns. On weekends, he generally spends the evenings out. His grandfather was a rip-roaring drinker, his father abstemious.

"My dad had Severn water in his veins," says Eustace, as if that made alcohol unnecessary. On Saturday nights, Eustace—who likes a pint or two—goes with a few friends to a pub or social club in one village or another not far from Ironbridge. On Friday nights during the winter, he is generally to be found with the Tontine domino team, either at the Tontine or at whatever pub they have gone to for an away match. There are many trophies for winning dominoes matches on the sideboard in one of the front rooms. Eustace says modestly, "There's a saying, 'There's no champion at dominoes'—but we've had a fair team over the years." Robin Long, the manager of the Tontine, praises the Tontine team but is still somewhat bemused by their earnestness. "You'd think they were playing chess," he says. "It seems to me that if you have five dominoes and only one will go, you have to play it."

Eustace was complaining about his back on the last morning of my stay. I ran into him in the market square near the Tontine and was strolling with him down to his house when an acquaintance hailed him: "How are you, then, Eustace?" "Not so good—the back," said Eustace. "What've you been doing, then?" "Nothing." Eustace turned to me, as we walked on. He said, "You don't have to be doing anything special for a back to come on." I agree. My back once went when I was lifting a toothbrush to my teeth. "I remember my father," Eustace continued, "getting out of a coracle after his back let go." Eustace grimaced as if the pain had been his.

Eustace and I had been talking obliquely about the voyage I wanted to make in my coracle. Perhaps because he did not consider me as yet sufficiently experienced in handling the craft, Eustace mentioned various problems I might face with weirs, floodwaters, rapids, and power-station inlets. Now he said, "The trouble with a longer voyage is the sitting—it's hard on the back." In his own case, he blames his lumbar pains mostly on a life on the land: few farm workers escape back problems, what with the humping of hay and straw, cattle feed and manure, the making of stacks and moving of milk churns. In his case, too, there was often the carrying home at night of a string of twenty rabbits over his shoulders, a weight of seventy pounds or so.

When we reached the shed, Eustace said, "Shall I show you how I handle the coracle?" Despite his morning back, Eustace brought out a coracle. "This is my own, a fraction smaller than yours." His coracle did not have a name; it was simply Eustace's coracle, like Eustace's jacket or Eustace's handsaw, as necessary as a piece of clothing or a tool for work. He looked like a large mushroom walking as he carried it over his head down the steep slope to where his open box-like raft lay against the bank, held by chains that allowed it to rise and fall with the level of the river.

The Severn was running strongly. Several ducks bore witness to this, swimming slowly across the current while being whisked downstream. "Everything is tricky about handling the coracle," said Eustace, after he had dropped it into the water alongside the raft and was holding it in place with the blade of his paddle. "My old man didn't mind tumbling in. If he upset, and was in deep water where he could get no footing, he'd rock his way in over the seat. I've seen him standing with his feet on the gunwale, one on each side, paddling from up there. I've never gone in for the acrobatics." Very smoothly, Eustace bent over and held the thwart of the coracle with one hand, while with the other he pressed the paddle inside the raised edge of the raft, keeping the coracle hard against the raft. He stepped in, sat down, and was off upstream toward the bridge at surprising speed, given that the water he was moving over was going the other way. He sat with his black boots planted a foot or so apart, pointing straight ahead. He leaned forward slightly, his left shoulder higher than his right, holding the top of the paddle with his left hand while with the right he held the loom about a third of the way down toward the blade, stirring the water as easily as one might stir a cup of tea. Then he spun and came out into midstream, paddling one-armed now, which was the way coracle men navigated their craft when laying eel lines or working a net, the loom of the paddle pressed against the inside of his right arm, making the paddle almost an extension of the arm. In midstream he returned to the two-handed grip, tackling for a moment the full strength of the current, slicing the blade to one side then the other in graceful arcs, the end of each arc taking the form of a little flick to the rear before the paddle—not leaving the water—swished forward and to the other side again. Twin whirlpools appeared and passed down each side of the coracle. Eustace darted once more across the river and then returned. As he climbed out onto the raft, he said, "You'll need to get lots of practice before you go on Severn."

In early May, I began to keep a more than usually interested eye on the weather charts in newspapers and on television. British weather is generally dominated by "lows," depressions moving in sequence eastward across the Atlantic, bringing rain, low clouds, and—if we're lucky—fitful sunny periods to illuminate our lush green grass. Now and again, however, the Azores high-pressure zone will swell out to embrace us, or part of it will seem to break off and squat unmoving for several splendid days or even more splendid weeks over these islands, while the sun shines and shines. What weather for a maiden Severn voyage a spell like that would make! More specifically, I needed days when—according to the lore of the Rogerses—rain had not been teeming down in North Wales, provoking a Severn spate. But I nevertheless felt the need to earmark a mid-May week in the family calendar for the expedition, so that other commitments did not impinge, and when it came to it, the calendar ruled that it was now—or not for another month or so. Margot and I decided to set off despite the unsettled weather forecast for the week. I made a Sunday-night phone call to Robin Long at the Tontine (Eustace is not on the phone) and was reassured with his report that the Severn was "quite low and stable." However, on the Monday morning, as we drove northward out of London, with the coracle lashed to the car roof rack and our headlights on, heavy rain was falling, to the accompaniment of a thick easterly gale. One bright note was that the rain was said to be coming down in diminished quantities in Wales.

The coracle upside down on top of the car has a reasonably aerodynamic shape and a benign effect on other drivers; they often smile when they notice it and occasionally—if overtaking—slow down, pull in behind for a moment, and have a closer look. Resting in our Greenwich garden for several days, it attracted cats, who sat and stared at it, climbed under it, and perhaps thought it was a new sort of birds' nest. I had been storing it in a shed beside a canal basin in Essex (where I generally moor a larger boat for sailing in the Blackwater estuary and the North Sea), and there, on the canal and an adjacent flooded gravel pit, I had got in some of the practice that Eustace had suggested—sometimes with Daisy aboard, sometimes without. Although she would have liked to accompany us northward, she did not.

Shrewsbury, a Shropshire town famous for its medieval and Tudor buildings, turned out to be full of visitors for the West Midlands agricultural show. Defoe said of Shrewsbury (which the locals pronounce "Shoosbry"): "They all speak English in the town, but on market day you would think you were in Wales." This is still the case. The women have sharply pretty faces. The men are stocky, complacent-cheeked, and look like farmers. The hotels were jammed, but we eventually found a room in a small guesthouse; the bed sagged, the mattress was soft. During an uneasy night, there were moments when, asleep or awake, I had visions of a surging, tumultuous river. I was up early next morning—overcast, but not raining or blowing—and tried to limber up with a walk along the riverfront. The Severn loops around the center of Shrewsbury, almost making an island of it; a long stretch of the river is lined with parks and public gardens, furnishing a number of points where coracle launching looked possible. The water seemed calm and not particularly fast-moving—or so I thought at first. Fortunately, I walked a little farther, and the current gave the impression of accelerating. I walked under a road bridge, the eighteenth-century English Bridge, which provides the town's eastern approach (the Welsh Bridge serves it from the west). I walked under a railway bridge, still following the river, with Shrewsbury Station and Castle on the slopes above, and heard, ahead, a steady roar that had nothing to do with trains. As it passed around a long bend, the river was now moving like a transparent glacier, but at far greater speed, and I came to the source of the sound: a weir, spanning the river, over which the waters of the Severn fell in a loud, constant cadence. It was a fall of three or four feet, perhaps; no Niagara. But I stood there, trying to imagine going over that smooth and glistening chute in a coracle.

We launched my basket craft an hour later, about half a mile farther on. Castle Field was the spot, a municipal open space by which the river flowed, with suburban houses standing above the far bank, and a small island just downstream, dividing the Severn's waters. Here the noise of the weir was a muted rumble. An elderly man walking by with his dog expressed interest; he hadn't seen a coracle in many years. We launched at a place where the grassy bank shelved gently to a muddy foreshore. I was wearing short rubber sea boots, corduroys, long-sleeved shirt, sweater, beret, and a thin waistcoat-type buoyancy aid. Tied beneath the thwart was a small waterproof bag containing a piece of calico, a tube of bitumen cement, a clasp knife, a pocket compass, a one-and-a-quarter-inch-to-a-mile ordnance map, notebook, pen, can of beer, and bar of chocolate. My orange foul-weather jacket lay behind the thwart; the morning, at 10 a.m., remained misty. I got the coracle into water just deep enough so that it wouldn't ground as my weight went into it. Margot held a line I had made fast to the coracle's gunwale, and I pressed the blade of the paddle into the river bottom just beyond the coracle, so that it did not slide away. Crouching low, I stepped in and seated myself on the very middle of the thwart, wondering how long my aching back was going to last at this. "See you in Atcham, I hope," I said to Margot, who was planning to drive there and paint watercolors at a spot where a bridge crosses the Severn and a hotel stands, a possible roof for the night. "When?" she asked. "I'm not sure," I replied. "Maybe a few hours."

The moment of letting go was similar, I imagine, to how it is with a balloon. The coracle swayed and bobbed and was lifted off on the current—not snatched, not thrust; the movement was immensely natural and easy. The river was not moving as fast as I had feared. Margot strolled along, keeping abreast of me, until she came to the end of Castle Field, and waved goodbye. I didn't have to work the paddle strenuously, but did so to keep the coracle heading in the right direction and more or less in midstream. I could tell how fast I was going through the water—as opposed to with it—by flecks of May blossoms and brown-white bubbles of foam which floated downriver, too, and provided markers, allowing me to see if I was simply floating at the same pace as them. If this was the case, I would be shamed into paddling the coracle constantly in order to overtake them. For the moment, I had the pleasant feeling of sharing the same buoyant, liberal element as the blossoms, the bubbles, and a pair of ducks sidling across the river. The Severn banks were here twelve to fifteen feet high, partly grassed, partly bare earth; hedges angled toward the banks, along the tops of which small willows and other tenuous shrubbery grew. My chief vista lay ahead, where the river afforded a longer prospect—as far, at least, as a modern road bridge. The traffic passing over it struck me as perversely out of place and absurd. As I approached the bridge, a small boy on a bicycle, going across, saw me coming and stopped. He leaned over the rail and waved, calling down: " 'Ow far 'ave you been?" Not far, I answered truthfully; and I didn't like to say how far I meant to go. I passed under the deep shadows of the bridge, and did some agile sculling to avoid water dripping from a pipe suspended beneath it.

The ordnance map told me that the river passed through the northern suburbs of Shrewsbury; but, with the bridge behind, my outlook was entirely rural. Cows on the right bank, some of whom paused amid their chewing to glance phlegmatically at me; a few anglers, who gave me slightly unbelieving stares and then rather suspicious nods or waves in reply to my greetings; birds in the trees and bushes making a constant susurrus of chitter, tweet, and chirp. Another background sound was that of water running in through numerous gullies and sluices in the banks. The river water looked browny-gray, though this gave the impression of being beneath a surface reflection which was browny-green. About half an hour after my departure, I reckoned from the map that I had covered a mile; this did not seem substantial. I took longer spells at sculling and pretty soon was doing it without thinking about it, no longer looking at the blade as I moved it in the water. The coracle wriggled forward, shimmying in a short arc—in clock-face terms, between 11 p.m. and 1 a.m. When I paused, resting the paddle across the rim and putting up each foot in turn in a restricted stretch, the coracle revolved slowly; it provided a handier means of seeing in all directions than a canoe or rowboat would have done. If I let it drift too long, however, it tended toward a bank, one of the river's immutable laws apparently being that sooner or later everything that floated on it would collide with one edge or the other. What wind there was seemed to be mostly astern, though the long sinuous bends sometimes brought it abeam. I recalled old wisdom about rivers—for instance, that the water moves fastest, and is deepest, on the outside of a bend. Although it was still gray, the sun behind the mist was beginning to warm the day. Another island divided the river, and just before I reached it, the water became shallow and bubbly. I recognized the significance of scale: the coracle had about three inches of freeboard forward, four inches at the side; any disturbance on the surface of the water looked threatening—a four-inch wave could be disastrous. But we bounced through the choppy patch. I followed a sequence of little vortexes into calmer water. Four swans swam ahead of me, now and then turning to spread their wings, as if to let me know they were decidedly there; but then, not yet seeking a showdown, swimming on.

I had been going about an hour and a half and was beginning to feel the need to stand straight when I came round the top of a large U-bend and saw several houses, a church tower, and a barn beside the river. This was the hamlet of Uffington. Two ladies were standing on a lawn which came to the riverbank, waving—I realized—at me. One called out: "Perhaps you would like to land here. Your wife said to look out for you." I clambered stiffly ashore, and slowly unbent. I tied the coracle to a stake. Margot, it seemed, had driven here, walked down what looked like a footpath to the river, found this house, and told its astonished but hospitable owner, Mrs. Brereton, that I was coming by in a coracle. Margot had then driven on to Atcham. Mrs. Brereton, a widow, was in the middle of cooking brunch for some visitors, an old school friend (the other lady) and her family, back from Australia for a holiday. The coracle amazed them. Mrs. Brereton said one hadn't been seen in Uffington for ten years or so. I declined a plate of bacon, sausage, eggs, and fried bread, and accepted, gratefully, a cup of coffee.

We talked for twenty minutes about coracles and about Australia. Mrs. Brereton said that there had once been a ferry here at Uffington across the river. Then I gave them my thanks and made my departure. My back felt restored—in fact, despite Eustace's warnings, it seemed remarkably improved by coracling.

The river's course was now southward, though still sinuously so. Near a bridge that carries a railway from Shrewsbury to Wellington, two boys, maybe eleven years old, were on the riverside path below an extensive field. One called out, very politely, "Excuse me, what's that you're in?" "A coracle." "A coracle?" "Yes." "Oh. Ta." Below the bridge, I passed a floating orange life buoy marked "Shrewsbury & Atcham District Council"—thrown in, I judged (perhaps unfairly), not to a swimmer in peril but for fun, by a youth feeling antisocial. The river was generally free of contemporary flotsam in the form of plastic bottles and chunks of Styrofoam. Here, at ten to one, a light rain began to fall; for ten minutes or so I wore my foul-weather jacket. And here, not far below the bridge, the river began to speed up again. Suddenly I could see the bottom—stones appeared, and long green strands of underwater plants billowed downstream. Another realization: of course, the river ran fastest in the shallow stretches, more slowly in the long, deep pools. Here I would need my wits about me. Not far ahead, the Severn foamed and crinkled. An angler stood nearly halfway across the river, with the water up to calf level on his gray-green rubber waders. Snags and rocks were apparent. This was Preston Boats, where there also used to be a ferry and—until 1910—the last fish weir spanned the Severn—a palisade of oak piles and wattles, from which eel nets were operated. Barges were hauled up a gutter or channel behind the man-made island near the west bank. I had to make a rapid decision. I aimed for the part of the old weir where the water looked smoothest, just about reached it, bumped slightly, felt a small splash come aboard, and was then over and abruptly in a back eddy, which took a good deal of paddle work to get out of. I had been too occupied to greet the angler, and he looked startled as I came bouncing past.

I also surprised two horses. They were a handsome pair, one black, one chestnut, and they cantered the long length of a field, following me. Across the river, sheep baaed as I passed. Ducks and moorhens scurried to each side, and swallows zoomed over. The river sauntered again and I sculled rhythmically. But it was a long last hour to Atcham, which I had hopes of reaching before the bar and restaurant of the hotel closed at 3 p.m. The noise of traffic indicated that the river was coming close to the A5 main road to and from Shrewsbury. I could see the tops of big trucks behind the trees and bushes along the right-hand bank. And at last I glimpsed Atcham road bridge, where the river makes a right-angle bend. Premature thoughts of landfall overwhelmed me —the river was in fact accelerating again. It broke into two streams, the narrowest of which funneled behind an island, the broader flow heading more directly for the bridge. I picked the broader stream and picked wrongly; the coracle bucked, crunched, and came to a halt. The gravel bottom was a few inches below the surface. I put one boot over and transferred a little of my weight out of the coracle. It bumped forward a few feet and came to a solid stop. I had to step out altogether and wade for several yards, towing the coracle, reboarding when I judged there was enough water to float again

Mermaid, a lofty Georgian house, it was once called
the Talbot; a mermaid figured in the coat of arms of the
Talbots, a local family, and, had one swum up the
Severn, might well have figured in the life of Jack
Mytton, a local rake, who on one occasion for a wager
rode a bear into the hotel. Mytton was a passionate
huntsman who drank up to half a dozen bottles of port
a day; he died in prison at the age of thirty-eight, and
three thousand people came to his funeral. Two coracles
were among the fishing gear he had owned, auctioned
after his death. Although the Mytton and Mermaid was
accommodating some of Shrewsbury's agricultural show
overspill, we found a comfortable room with a slightly
firmer bed than the previous night's. In the late afternoon, when I had recovered from the morning's exercise, Margot and I drove to Wroxeter, five minutes by
car—a hamlet where several fields near the Severn have
been excavated to reveal some of the ruins of the Roman
city of Viroconium or Uriconium, capital of the province
of Britannia Secunda and in its heyday, c. 250, the fourth-
largest city in the British Isles. A fine rain was falling
on the green turf which has replaced paths and roads
between ancient foundations, exposed hypocausts, the
floors of the baths, the bases of sixteen stone pillars (once
part of the Forum), and alongside a still-upstanding
section of rough wall, believed to have been part of the
municipal granary. Viroconium was abandoned with the
withdrawal of the Legions in 410 and provided ready-
to-hand building material for the growing settlement of
Shrewsbury in Anglo-Saxon times. Sheep were nibbling
the grass over the former Forum. A few miles to the
east, the horizon rose in an abrupt upheaving—a hill,
looking like an extinct volcano or sleeping beast, called

the Wrekin (a word, like Wroxeter, derived from a British version of Viroconium). A. E. Housman was here, presumably on an autumn day, and wrote the poem that begins:

> *On Wenlock Edge the wood's in trouble;*
> *His forest fleece the Wrekin heaves;*
> *The gale, it plies the saplings double,*
> *And thick on Severn snow the leaves.*
>
> *'Twould blow like this through holt and hanger*
> *When Uricon the city stood:*
> *'Tis the old wind in the old anger,*
> *But then it threshed another wood.*

Two days of rain had got the Severn moving fast next morning across the shallows below the Atcham bridges. The master of one of the local hunts was drowned here, twenty years or so ago, when trying to ford the river during a late-autumn spate. Nevertheless, the anglers were up early in quest of the elusive salmon; several stood out on the shoal, with their lines cast out into the pool, while one elderly man sat on a primitive two-legged stool planted in the bank where St. Eata's grave-yard came to the river's edge. He walked over to watch me prepare the coracle for launching, and perhaps to see if I had a salmon net aboard. He had fished here for forty years, he said, and had never seen a coracle—was thrilled to see one, and wanted to know how to work it. In answer to the questions I put to him, in return, he said that he had *seen* a salmon half an hour before.

It was a finer day, already warmer, but with a blustery south wind. I hoped to get to Cressage, eight miles on, and to a hotel called the Old Hall, where Margot meant to meet me. Once out of the rapid current below Atcham, I had some hard paddling dead to windward. I felt the gaze of the anglers on my back and couldn't disappoint them. You might think that the river current would carry one forward despite a headwind, but this is not the case—the coracle's grip on the water is so small; it rides on the water like a piece of fluff and can be blown back over the current, especially when furnished with the extra windage of a person in it. I crouched as low as I could while still wielding the paddle. I tried a variety of techniques that I had worked out the day before, particularly a shorter, sharper sculling stroke, twisting the paddle over the bow so that it acted more like a propeller, rotating one way, then the other. But once out of view of the anglers I sought the right-hand bank and held onto a willow bough for a few minutes to get my breath back. Some of the new green leaves of the willow were underwater, evidence of a higher Severn. A group of swans—perhaps the same as yesterday's—was doing better than I at making progress downstream.

An eastward reach came next, however, and rewarded my labors. I stayed in the lee of the right-hand bank, and the wind, on the beam, was mostly in my hair. For a while, too, the river narrowed and the pace of the current increased. I aimed for the smooth areas of the swirling water ahead. With the chance to spin round, at the flick of the paddle, I saw behind me up on a ridge a fine Regency house. Cronkhill was its name, according to the indispensable Ordnance Survey; white stucco, and with a domed black roof on a tower section (the sort of house that one covets in *Country Life* advertisements). Ahead, still spinning, I glimpsed the Wrekin for the first time from the river; the sun—exactly at 11 a.m.—began to appear. But these benefits were immediately countered by the wind as I came into a short north-south stretch and found I could make no progress whatever. I was blown backward faster than I could impel the coracle forward. I made for the left bank and hooked the paddle blade into the reeds. I sat, bobbing in the little waves, waiting for a lull and admiring the yellow-green glow of a vast field of rape—one felt it would show up like a radium watch dial in the dark. When the wind eased for a moment, I made a dash for the slightly more protected shore opposite, where there was also a more gently shelving bank. Here I disembarked and towed the coracle for a quarter of a mile. A white domestic duck gone native watched me getting mud high on my boots. When I climbed back aboard, for another long, unhindered spell, I made good use of the sponge which I'd added to the coracle's basic equipment.

In this stretch, I made a simple navigational error of a sort that the enormous loops of the river, and the exertion, may have contributed to. I saw a church tower across the fields and thought, "Wroxeter Church—I'm making good progress." But the sun wasn't quite where it should have been if that was the case. Indeed, my compass told me the church bore due west—not east, as Wroxeter's would. It was Atcham Church still. And this was confirmed by the realization that I had only got as far as the point where the River Tern joined the Severn. It poured in from the north, its brown-gravy-colored waters remaining for a long way visibly independent (as the waters of the Missouri remain many miles after joining the Mississippi). The Tern's extra flow gave me greater momentum. Along here, I caught up with the swans again; there were a dozen of them now, and they decided they weren't going any farther. They all turned round to face me. They spread their wings and began to beat them. Then they took off, right for me, a white-winged squadron, buffeting the air just above my head. I ducked, though I didn't need to. The noise encouraged two Canada geese to fly away too, though with less menace. Other birds to be seen were several black-headed gulls, many rooks, blackbirds, wood pigeons, swallows, and thrushes. I heard and then saw a single cuckoo and later watched the leisurely takeoff of a gray heron, an equally solitary bird. I also heard a big splash near the bank and glimpsed in a cascade of water the pink-gray snout of what I felt sure was a salmon.

At Wroxeter, the river went due south for more than a mile with Roman directness. Fortunately, there was a long island at the beginning of this stretch, and I chose or was taken into the narrower, more easterly channel. This was the right choice for depth of water, speed of current, and shelter from the wind. (Later I read that most of these islands were man-made at places where the river was shoal and where there were fords and weirs; the narrow channels behind the islands were created for hauling through barges, and the islands themselves furnished places where cargo could temporarily be unloaded to lighten the barges.) Here the Roman road called Watling Street had crossed the river. A white modern house stood near the river, a prosperous assortment of laundry billowing on a line in the garden, and a small red motorboat tied up to a little jetty—the first boat I'd seen. Wroxeter Church tower appeared in the trees behind.

It was a workout thereafter. For distraction, I had a compulsory passage under some power lines spanning the river. I could hear them crackle. I wondered whether high-tension electricity ever jumped downward, perhaps finding a coracle paddle in the water a convenient ground or earth. I let my mind linger on the names of several nearby villages, such as Eaton Constantine and Cross Houses; there is no doubt some houses do look cross. I decided that if anyone again asked what I was doing I would answer that I was waiting for the invention of the oar. I kept my windage low and promised myself I would stop for lunch when I reached the end of this stretch. But I had not quite done so when, at 1 p.m., I paddled to the left bank and tied the coracle to a willow bough. I climbed the red-brown earth, getting a purchase from shrubs and clumps of grass. I spread my foul-weather jacket over a patch of nettles at the edge of a big field sown with young wheat. The wind was noisy, shaking the nettles, grass, and trees, and making little wavelets as it slapped against the current. In the margin between field and river, there were not only grass and nettles but flowers: daisies and bluebells, buttercups and dandelions, speedwell and vetch, celandine and campion. I ate a cold meat pie, a doughnut, and an apple. I drank a small can of beer. Then I lay back in the warmth of the sun and let my aching shoulders, elbows, and wrists go flop for ten minutes. I looked up at willow boughs and sky.

Restored, I reembarked at one-thirty. Past Caton's Farm, past sheep on the banks, sculling hard I made the end of the stretch and coasted around a bend under the shelter of the south bank. Another stream came in here —Cound Brook, draining the lands of Candover and Cantlop, Eaton Mascott and Cound. On the opposite bank, the landscape was novel. The river ran at the foot of a forty-foot-high stone cliff, red-gray, with trees here and there growing out of deep fissures in the rock. This was Eyton, with an ancient tower—not visible, but shown on the map—which I took to be part of the ancestral home of the Herberts. Lord Herbert of Cherbury, born here, was the brother of George Herbert the poet, and was himself a poet, philosopher, autobiographer, ambassador, linguist, and musician, and a good friend of Ben Jonson and John Donne. Lord Herbert is buried in St. Giles-in-the-Fields Church, in London, where Andrew Marvell also lies. In the poetry of coracles, one must recall the last lines of Marvell's "Upon Appelton House":

> *But now the* Salmon-Fishers *moist*
> *Their* Leathern Boats *begin to hoist;*
> *And, like* Antipodes *in Shoes,*
> *Have shod their* Heads *in their* Canoos.
> *How* Tortoise *like, but not so slow,*
> *These rational* Amphibii *go?*
> *Let's in: for the dark* Hemisphere
> *Does now like one of them appear.*

At the south end of this cliff, three men stood on the bank, with tall trees behind: two of them elderly, looking like gamekeepers; one, in his thirties, fishing. (The fishing on the river is generally privately owned, proclaimed as such by bankside notices, and is rented out by landowners to fishing clubs from which permits have to be bought.) One of the older men called out, "What are you doing up this way?"

He obviously recognized an Ironbridge coracle, and deserved a more serious answer than the one I'd thought of giving about the invention of the oar. I said, "I'm going down the river from Shrewsbury. I left Atcham this morning."

The fisherman called out, "Did I see you at Atcham Bridge yesterday?"

"Yes."

"With your wife, weren't you?"

toward the foot of the Wrekin. Here, the railway line that Harry Rogers and Nacky followed is now part of the hotel grounds; the tracks have been dismantled, but a railway semaphore-type signal stands in a side yard. The Old Hall has a spacious restaurant and limited accommodations—only five bedrooms; its new owners were away on holiday. Margot got there to find an electrician at work and a girl named Karen in sole charge of the establishment. But she agreed to lodge and feed us, the only guests, and she found a board to put under the mattress (which Margot judged to be not quite firm enough for the coracle traveler) of the bed in the Wrekin Room (which Margot chose instead of the Moat, Rose, Castle, or Severn rooms). I found myself helping the electrician discover why the light over our bed was glowing when the switch was off (water dripping into a junction box from a leaking radiator in an attic room), and I discovered for him how the nonoperational fan in the bar could be made to function. When Karen couldn't get the furnace going (and the repairman couldn't be reached), I spent fifteen minutes pressing various buttons and fiddling with contacts and switches and got it started, so there was hot water for baths that night. Margot was equally busy, talking to the vegetable delivery man, making tea in the kitchen, and shooing out of the elegant front hall a pair of white ducks who kept walking in through the open door from the garden. Karen cooked me one of the best bacon-eggs-sausages-tomatoes-mushrooms-fried-bread breakfasts I've ever had. We had a feeling of being needed—of being more than guests— and were sorry when we had to leave. In a nearby pub, we met the elderly fisherman I had passed above the bridge, and he apologized for not having responded to what, on reflection, he recognized as my greeting. When he fished, he always turned off his hearing aid. He wanted to know about the coracle.

On the third morning, the top of the Wrekin was mist-shrouded, but as seen from the bay window of the Wrekin Room, at seven o'clock, the limpid grays and greens of bridge, river, and meadows had an imperma-nent air: the climbing sun would burn off the mistiness and sharpen the colors. It was going to be a splendid, nearly windless day. When I launched the coracle next to Cressage Bridge at nine-forty, the air was just moist, however, with little shudders—mere wisps of breeze—disturbing it now and then. Words like "zephyr" seemed appropriate; "sylvan" and "sward" were others that came to mind. Filaments of gossamer drifted through the air. Because I was afloat now on what I thought of as Eustace's waters and had a perhaps unreasonable con-fidence in my coracle-handling ability, I left my buoy-ancy waistcoat in the bottom of the craft, behind the thwart. But I knew the river would do a lot of the work for me today and I let it carry me contemplatively at first while I got into my sculling stride—on a long stretch west-east, then a sharp, exciting bend northward with a strong back eddy to be avoided, at the outside elbow of the bend. The current suddenly shot me along among bunched bubbles of foam.

Other elements of my passage that morning were similar to those of the previous two days, albeit intensi-fied by the beneficent weather and, perhaps, also by the sense that this was the concluding stage, so that I looked at birds and plants and water, and listened to natural sounds, with the greater attention of one who must shortly relinquish these pleasures. I was, as well, among the names and places Eustace had talked of, landmarks for the Rogerses. I was looking at fields and woods where the rabbits had been trapped and was passing over waters where salmon nets and eel lines had been laid, while landowners and gamekeepers raged on the banks. The perfection of the pastoral was here, at Leighton—as close to the Wrekin as the Severn comes, though the view of the little mountain is made intermittent by copses planted along the sloping riverfront. A fine eighteenth-century brick mansion stands amid terraced lawns and surrounding parkland, bringing to mind Eustace's "old man Kynnersley," who had lived in the house. (Another Leighton person was Mary Webb, born in the village in 1881, author of *Gone to Earth* and other novels that had a vogue in the 1920s, and perhaps—with those of D. H. Lawrence—inspired Stella Gibbons to her comic parody of the genre, *Cold Comfort Farm*.) Sheep browsed on Leighton side among gorse and Michaelmas daisies while Cuyp-like golden cows munched in the low pastures across the river. Canada geese patrolled with their young along the bank. I saw a salmon jump as I drifted round the bend beneath the woods of Cockshut Rough, and sculling close to a dead tree that had fallen out into the river, I got within ten feet of a fox. He was standing out over the water on a bough, red-brown, sharp-eared, with something black and floppy in his mouth. When he saw me, he gave me a look that suggested I had no right to have got so close to him, before he trotted onto the bank and into the trees.

A massive landmark now rose ahead, signaling the end of the river's leisurely bends through water meadows and the beginning of the hills through which it passed more narrowly and deeply: Buildwas Power Station. What one sees from some way upstream is its tall single chimney and four immense cooling towers, bulging from the power station a loud digestive rumble, which went on for thirty seconds and suddenly stopped—perhaps the sound of coal being engorged; at least, not core meltdown. The place had—with its disproportionate scale and apparent lack of human beings working there —a slightly eerie interest. This had struck Margot, too. After I'd been underway for five minutes, I saw her on the bank opposite the power station, finishing a sketch. I stopped to say hello and coordinate our movements in this last segment of the voyage; it was now a little less than two miles to Ironbridge. When I set off again, she walked more or less abreast of me along the riverside path, where it existed, and where it did not she scrambled through a hedge and followed the road below Coalbrookdale. Several bridges belonging to the power station gave access for road trucks and rail wagons carrying coal; power cables sizzled overhead; great clouds of white steam rose from the earth-goddess-shaped cooling towers; and a continuous murmur came from a building beside the river I recognized as the water inlet plant where Eustace had worked in the days before the cooling towers were built. Fortunately, no suction effect—drawing the coracle that way—was perceptible. But I sculled hard, keen to put these industrial fascinations behind me, and making Margot hurry to keep me in sight.

In a few minutes, I had rounded the bend below the overhanging woods of Benthall Edge, on the right bank. On the left bank, the road ran into Ironbridge along a riverside terrace, over whose iron railing visitors peered down to look at the Severn, and, seeing me, to wave. I waved back at them with the paddle, and the coracle took a liberated spin—which I hoped the spectators knew was perfectly intentional on my part. The river twisted slightly again, and ahead I could see the iron bridge, spun across the gorge like a substantial cobweb. From the river surface, the gorge seemed deep; the houses of the village were stacked high, one above the other. I could see the third floor and roof of the Tontine, where Margot and I intended to have lunch. The river was running faster. I gave myself a firm order to concentrate now, in these last minutes, for I didn't want to tumble in, here of all places, or botch my landing. Nor did I want to spoil my sculling style by being too conscious of it. I could see a number of people standing on the bridge, and seeing me coming, they beckoned to others to let them know there was something of interest down below. My attention was momentarily taken by a spark of metallic blue that seemed to burst from the river like an electric flash and streak away: a kingfisher. Then I was under the bridge, passing under the center of the arch, and I could see Eustace's shed, the bank up to his front garden, and Eustace himself, in shirtsleeves and pullover, clipping the front hedge, his back to the river. I called out "Eustace!" as I sculled toward the bank from midstream, allowing, I hoped, for the downriver set. For a moment I thought that Eustace, without looking, was going to have an attack of shyness and take to his house; there was a suspicion of movement that way. Then he turned and saw me. He put down the shears, came down the bank, and stood watching me as I sculled vigorously over the last few yards of current to his raft.

"You've had a good day for it, haven't you?" he said, looking really pleased to see me and the coracle he had made. "How did you like the little boat?" And then, before I could answer him, or express my own feelings of well-being, he added his accolade: "You've done very well."